JOYFUL COPY

How to Show Up in the Marketplace
Ethically and Authentically

JOY CAPPS

(aka Joy Capps Parrish)

Joyful Copy

How to Show Up in the Marketplace Ethically and Authentically

by

Joy Capps
(aka Joy Capps Parrish)

ISBN: 979-8-9860108-0-9

Published by Engaging Business Communications, LLC
JoyCapps.com

Book Cover Design and Artwork
Aasman Iqbal, Art Director, Front Foot Advertising, Islamabad, Pakistan
thefrontfoot.com.pk/our-team/

Editing, Interior Formatting and Layout Services
Affordable Christian Editing Services
affordablechristianediting.com
Published in the United States of America

DEDICATION

This book is dedicated to my Business Partner, Abba Father, whose mercy, grace, and love are never-ending. Thank you for your ongoing patience with me as you've transformed my life. I will spend eternity thanking and praising You for guiding me towards the many ways to shine Your Light in the world and marketplace. Thank you for showing me how to use the Bible as the Ultimate How-To manual in partnership with Holy Spirit as my guide. May this book you called me to write help every person who reads it.

ACKNOWLEDGMENTS

With heartfelt gratitude and thanks:

To my parents, Rev. Van and Patsy Capps, who consistently modeled how to have a personal relationship with Jesus, thank you for the incredible blessing of being your daughter.

To my husband, Robert, whose constant love, encouragement, prayers, and support help me pursue the dreams God has placed on my heart—I could not do what I do without you by my side cheering me on.

To Shae Bynes, thank you for being God's conduit and revealing how to partner with Abba Father genuinely. This book would not have come to life without your guidance. Thank you for challenging, pushing, and encouraging me to write this book while pursuing God's heart.

To my friend and colleague, Kim Krajci, thank you for your consistent input and support as I've walked this journey. You are a rare jewel and blessing. Thank you for the honor of your friendship.

To my friends, colleagues, and clients who have provided me with feedback, encouragement, and support as I've helped you plan strategic communications, execute marketing, create and write copy, and provide values-based coaching for your businesses and lives.

FOREWORD

As a mentor and teacher who has spent the past decade helping entrepreneurs partner with God in business and align with the mindset, heart, and ways of Jesus Christ, I have been eagerly awaiting a book like this.

After getting to know Joy Capps in the summer of 2019 as a participant in our Kingdom Driven Entrepreneur certification program, I sensed that my wait was coming to a close. Finally, I met someone skilled in copywriting who understood that biblical Scripture *and* the Holy Spirit serve as the best foundation and guide, plus had the heart to teach and equip others. I committed myself to stay the course with Joy and continue to advise and encourage her (gently and not so gently as she will verify) until I saw this book completed.

Copywriting (writing words that inform, educate, and persuade) is a key communication skill for business, and, for years, I have watched good-hearted and well-intentioned entrepreneurs either:

1. Fall into a trap of deception and manipulation simply because they were following the commonly taught "blueprints of success" in marketing and sales, or…

2. Fail to consistently market and sell their product and service offerings at all because their hearts could not align with what they saw as best practices, but they also did not have a resource to help them do it in a way that fully aligned with their values.

Joyful Copy is a copywriting masterclass in book form that offers theory and rich principles, and provides illustrations, examples, and guidance for practical application. It does not disregard industry wisdom and human psychology but provides a biblical framework and approach. However, the most powerful part is that it positions you to experience God's best in business by partnering with Him – the One who intimately knows you and everyone you're called to serve through the work you do. Enjoy the adventure!

Shae Bynes
Founder of Kingdom Driven Entrepreneur
Author of *Grace Over Grind* and *The Kingdom-Driven Entrepreneur's Guide: Doing Business God's Way*

CONTENTS

PREFACE:
BEFORE WE DIVE IN

Hi! I'm Joy, and I'm so glad you've picked up this book. If you're reading this preface, it probably means that you're an entrepreneur, small business owner, or marketer who wants to learn how to write words that connect with your customers without twisting reality.

The good news is that your desire for ethical marketing and joyful copywriting is indeed possible. Stick with me, and I'll share what I've learned that is counterintuitive to today's norm and how you can apply those principles to your business and life.

You may be at the beginning, middle, or "more senior" in your entrepreneurial journey. No matter what phase you're in, I wrote this book to help everyone seeking a better way to stand out in today's marketplace.

My ideal reader is someone who is already working and living life as a Christ-following entrepreneur. But I know that *anyone* will benefit from the principles found within these pages, no matter what you believe or what you're doing for a living.

Please know that what I've written is nothing new as I've pulled together concepts I've studied and continue to study from God's Word and various master copywriters. I have also pulled in specific concepts that Abba Father and Holy Spirit placed on my heart.

My standard operating procedure involves pairing practical marketing concepts with the teachings of the Bible. I do that by intentionally striving to make sure everything I write and speak aligns with God's Word. (It is something I work on every day because my human nature gets in the way all the time.)

It is important to know that I haven't always lived this way. While I accepted Jesus Christ as my personal Savior when I was six years old, I did not start consistently putting the Lord first in my life until I was in my 40s. And I didn't begin partnering with Abba Father in business until my 50s. Today, you'll find me starting each day asking Holy Spirit to fill me, renew me, and help me hear His voice in all I think, say, and do—and then taking action on it. (The 'taking action' part is critical. Because it is one thing to know something and another to do what you know to do.)

If you don't know the Good News already, please allow me to share with you that God sent His only Son to live on the earth among us, die on the cross for our sins, and rise from the dead three days later. Time and again, the Bible tells us that God sacrificed His Son to die for our sins because He loves us so much. And if you accept Jesus as your personal Savior by believing in Him and developing a personal relationship with Him, you will receive the gift of eternal life. (See John 3:16, Romans 10:9–10.)

If you haven't accepted Jesus as your personal Savior yet, now is a good time. All you need to do is talk to Him and invite Him into your life. Then take a stand each day to read the Bible, pray, and ask Him to help you navigate life.

Say something like this: Jesus, forgive me for trying to do life and business on my own. I believe that You died on the cross for my sins and rose from the dead three days later. I invite You into my life. Thank You for saving me and helping me to be more like You. Please help me to shine Your light brightly and authentically in the world. In Jesus' Name. Amen.

If you said that prayer, I want to encourage you to find a church and community of believers who study and practice **all** the teachings in the Bible. If you're not sure how to find the right group, send me an email at Joy@JoyCapps.com, and I'll do what I can to point you in the right direction.

You might wonder how I can do that if we don't live near each other. But using Google is one of my superpowers, so I'd be happy to use that superpower to help you.

Now, without further ado, let's dive into what God put on my heart to share with you.

Be blessed,

Joy

P.S. Before you move forward, I need to tell you one more thing. Sometimes when I use names of the Lord or the Trinity, I don't put the word "the" in front of them. If I did, it would be like saying or writing "the Kim" or "the Robert" when I call out to my friend or husband. Please know that when I write Abba Father, which I typically call God, or Holy Spirit–it is intentional because I'm addressing or speaking about someone very real to me and hopefully already is (or will become) very real to you, too.

INTRODUCTION:
"DO WHATEVER IT TAKES"

As a professional business communicator who spent many decades working for corporate America, agencies, and my own LLC—I've learned marketing, public relations, and copywriting skills at the feet of industry leaders, renowned entrepreneurs, and really smart people who excel at what they do.

While I have many unique and entertaining stories from my work with well-known brands like Compaq, Enron, and Stan Lee (yes, *that* Stan Lee)—I didn't realize until decades later that I invested way too much time focusing on the wrong things.

You see, the consistent drumbeat I learned to follow involved a "do whatever it takes" mentality to build brand awareness, create engagement, and increase the bottom line.

Simultaneously, I witnessed many of my superiors climb over others while stabbing people in the back in the name of "winning at all costs." Sometimes I saw friends and colleagues mistreated, and people stabbed me in the back at times.

While I excelled quickly, I was unaware that I was a naive pawn in the games others were playing. I had no idea that I was drinking how-to lessons from proverbial fire hoses filled with subtle hype and underhanded manipulation. I was surrounded by smoke and mirrors that focused on financial and customer growth with a strong undercurrent of personal gain for the "greater good."

What Held Me Back

Nothing in the strategies and tactics I learned to use so well ever aligned with God or the teachings of the Bible. In fact, I quickly found that talking about godly things in the workplace was shunned and discouraged. Over the years, many told me that Jesus had no place in business and to "leave that kind of talk at home." Seriously, I can't tell you the countless times I got in trouble for talking about Jesus.

Even though I was raised in a devout Christian home, I did not possess the wisdom or discernment to realize that focusing on "doing a good job," pleasing the higher-ups, and meeting key performance indicators (KPIs) was actually holding me back from my God-given destiny. Upon reflection, it is easy to see how every situation, opportunity, and experience pulled me deeper into the frenetic chaos.

Mired in a world where "everyone is doing it, so it must be alright," I didn't even realize that I'd lost sight of some of the values my parents taught me. However, my strong work ethic found me extremely focused on doing whatever I could to make those I worked for look good.

- Long hours? No problem.
- Twisting the truth with a bit of hype? Why not?!
- Sensationalism marketing and public relations? Sure thing.
- (Insert any outrageous, attention-getting tactic here?) Absolutely.

If it might work to generate results, I saw no reason not to try it. (Thankfully, I drew the line at breaking the law.)

Praying for the Wrong Favor

As the years went by and my career path allowed me to support some amazing projects and people, I kept trying to seek God and lean into Him for strength. While my intentions were good, my actions were far from perfect. If anything, I was living in a warped sense of reality that blurred the lines between worldly goals and Christianity.

Without realizing it, I innocently twisted my prayers when time and again, I asked God to give me favor with my employers, bosses, and clients. Everything I did was laser-focused on making clients and C-Suite execs happy while doing whatever was needed to help the bottom line of my employers or clients grow. (It wasn't until many years later that I would understand that the favor I needed was from God, not other humans.)

As I followed my career and supported my clients around the nation and globe, I had no idea I was sucked into the vortex of worldly ambitions and personal gain. Continuing to drink the proverbial Kool-Aid only kept me focused on the wrong things while helping me miss out on the many blessings I could have experienced along the way.

Life-Changing Catalysts

One life-changing event—where I had my foot rebuilt—forced me to unplug from the rat race just long enough for God to give me a glimpse of what I'd been missing. That catalyst, along with prompting from my husband Robert, found me taking the leap to jump full-time into my LLC by offering marketing, public relations, and copywriting services to businesses. But that was only the beginning of the changes God had in store for me.

As the years passed, one ongoing client situation turned sideways, and it became clear that they were subtly selling a form of vaporware and pipedreams. Their hidden quest was to bilk people out of large sums of money with no intention of fulfilling the actual promises they made during the sale. They did this with a smile on their face as they waved their version of a Jesus flag ever-so-slightly to attract marketplace Christians into their web. And here I was smack dab in the middle of it all—working as hard as possible to please this client. Yikes! Before I knew what happened, God used this situation as another tipping point and a catalyst to get my attention and change my course of direction.

Many years have passed, and I now see how Abba Father allowed these various circumstances to break my spirit, drive me to my knees, and shake my foundation. Why? He needed me to focus entirely on Him so that I would see everything through His viewpoint.

Nudges in the Right Direction

Years before the sideways client situation, I remember stumbling into a podcast called the *Kingdom Driven Entrepreneur*, and what this woman shared attracted me like a moth to a flame and pulled me in so quickly that it scared me a little. But it also seemed to fill my hunger for learning how to walk with God authentically, especially in today's business world.

Sadly, something would always divert my attention and get me to focus elsewhere before any of the concepts she shared could take root. This back-and-forth game happened so many times that I remember becoming annoyed at one point. Seriously?! As I look back, it is easy to see how Abba Father kept bringing me back to this particular ministry time and again. (Thank goodness He is patient.)

When I finally found myself committed to seeking God, Shae Bynes' Kingdom Driven Entrepreneur ministry reappeared in my line of sight yet again. And this time, I stuck around to hear what Abba had for me. From *Firestarter School* to *Igniters* to *Grace Over Grind*, I hungrily consumed every morsel of what God taught through her.

Seeing Things Through His Lens

For the first time in my life, I understood how to do life and business in partnership WITH God. This new-to-me process took the Christian foundation given to me as a child to heights I never knew existed.

As I learned how to hear Holy Spirit's voice, He showed me a better way to show up in today's marketplace. Step by step, He made it clear how today's Kingdom-Driven, Christ-following entrepreneurs need to stand out and connect with customers authentically.

- Bye-bye, hype and manipulation.
- Farewell, worldly ideals and goals.
- Adios, personal gain and self-focus.
- Sayonara, bait-and-switch tactics.
- Arrivederci to doing anything not aligned with the Bible.

In turn, I quietly started using this new-to-me method with my marketing clients without saying a word. The next thing I knew, God helped me clearly see a completely fresh perspective on copywriting and business coaching.

This approach was new to me because God gave me wisdom and discernment to use the marketing skills I already possessed in a way that aligned with the teachings of the Bible. (All the while, I kept thinking, "Who in business does this?!" But the more I leaned into Him, the more He revealed to me.)

What I now call joyful copy and values-based business coaching came to life in the Summer of 2019. Little did I know that God would use these insights that He helped me create—along with consistent nudging, guidance, and outright pushing from Shae Bynes—to write this very book.

My hope is that every person who reads this book will walk away with a new appreciation for and understanding of what it means to:

- Partner with God in business

- Align with the teachings of the Bible

- Take a stand to shine His light in a dark marketplace

- Write joyful copy that connects with customers without twisting reality

- Use the greatest how-to manual ever written (aka the Bible) with Holy Spirit as a guide

- Show up in the marketplace ethically and authentically

- And so much more

As you read through the following sections, I want to encourage you to stop and seek the Lord along the way. You may read new-to-you insights or see old ideas from a different perspective.

Whatever you do, please be intentional in asking God to guide you so that you find ways to shine His light authentically in today's marketplace.

How to Use This Book

I wrote the chapters of *Joyful Copy* sequentially to walk you through copywriting as it is used in the world today in concert with what God's Word says about how Christ-followers should show up in today's marketplace. While jumping around between sections and chapters might be tempting, I wrote the sequence to build one upon the other. Taken out of context or used without checking for alignment may produce results that are not considered joyful copy.

Reflection Questions

At the end of each chapter, you'll find questions designed to help you reflect on how you can apply what you've read to your life and business. It will be helpful for you to spend some time with those questions before you move on to the following chapters.

Consider using a journal or computer to record your responses. Then you can refer back to them often and update your thoughts as needed. While journaling will help you get your ideas out, reviewing what you've written will emphasize areas you want to work on and help you see growth.

Your Reservoir of Information

As you move through Part V: How to Determine Copy That Connects, you will encounter specific [ACTION STEPS] that are exercises you'll want to complete. These exercises will become your Reservoir of Information. You'll refer back to this information when you write joyful copy and in Part VI: Distill Joyful Copy: Connecting with Your Customers, so you'll want to keep your responses in an easy-to-access location.

Frameworks

You can apply joyful words to anything you do in life and business. From a business perspective, you'll want to use joyful copy on web pages and sales pages and in emails and social media posts. While I have many frameworks I could share, doing so could turn into standalone lessons, books, and courses; some of which I've already created, teach, and use for clients. In fact, many other marketers in the world have developed those things, too. Since the book already contains a great deal of information for you to work through and absorb— you'll find a handful of frameworks in Part VI to get you started.

Appendix

The appendix at the end of the book offers power tools and principles from each section.

The How-to Guide Power Tools

This will include my paraphrase of specific verses used in each chapter. While I wrote the paraphrases to emphasize what God placed on my heart, I strongly encourage you to read each verse in the actual Bible. I recommend that you read each verse in several translations to gain a deeper understanding of what they mean.

The translations I reference frequently include the New King James Version (NKJV), New International Version (NIV), and the Amplified Bible (AMP). On occasion, I'll also use The Message (MSG), the New Living Translation (NLT), and the Good News Translation (GNT). While everyone has reasons to favor one translation over another, I recommend you find what works best for you to understand what God is teaching through His Word (aka The Ultimate How-To Guide.)

The YouVersion Bible app, which is free, is accessible via the mobile app or your Internet browser at www.bible.com.

The Key Principles

The key principles from each chapter are listed for quick and easy reference. I encourage you to read through them periodically to keep them top of mind.

The Joyful Copy Challenge

Ultimately, *Joyful Copy* is a reminder and challenge to partner with God before you write, throughout the writing process, and after you've written. The *Joyful Copy* Checklist is a visual reminder to filter everything you write, think, and say through Galatians 5:22–23 and Philippians 4:8. Whenever a phrase or thought is out of alignment, the goal is to revise it until it emulates Christian characteristics.

Have Questions?

If you have questions about writing joyful copy, talk to God about it first. He may help you see what you need to change automatically. He may also point you to me. In that case, please email me at Joy@JoyCapps.com, and I'll get back to you as soon as possible.

INTRODUCTION: REFLECTION QUESTIONS

Before you move on to the next section, please take a moment to think about the following questions. You may want to consider journaling your responses, so you can refer back to them as we work through Joyful Copy (the book) together.

Points to Ponder

What has diverted your attention from reaching your God-given goals?

When it comes to marketing and copywriting your business, do you:

- Tend to follow what others do or make it up as you go along?
- Find the tasks overwhelming or difficult?

What steps do you currently take to build brand awareness, create engagement, and increase your bottom line?

Who do you partner with to get things done in your life and business? Why do you partner with them versus someone else?

Where does God rank in your list of partners?

Are you currently pursuing your God-given destiny? If yes, what does God have you doing? How is that working for you?

Do you pray for favor from your clients or God?

What situation(s) has Abba Father allowed to happen to get your attention? What lessons or insights have you gleaned from each experience?

PART I
WHAT IS COPY?

A few years ago, I spoke at a virtual summit about using copywriting to move from Joyless to Joyful. One question jumped out at me during the session: "Can you help me understand what copy is?"

This straightforward question reminded me that the concept of copywriting is not clear to everyone and could mean different things to different people. So, I think it is important that you and I spend a few moments looking at the concept to ensure we're singing from the same sheet of music.

To validate spending a moment clarifying the concept, I've noticed some people use "copywriting" and "copyrighting" interchangeably without realizing it. So, let's spend a moment unpacking both terms.

As a case in point, someone recently sent a note asking if I'd consider speaking at their upcoming conference about "copyrighting." While both terms look similar, "copyrighting" and "copywriting" are completely different concepts.

Merriam Webster defines the term "copyright" as "the exclusive legal right to reproduce, publish, sell, or distribute the matter and form of something (such as a literary, musical, or artistic work)."

While the definitions for copywriting vary from resource to resource, they collectively point to the art of writing words to sell, inform, and educate.

- The Oxford Dictionary defines copywriting as "the activity or occupation of writing the text of advertisements or publicity materials."

- Wikipedia states that "copy is written content that aims to increase brand awareness and persuade a person or group to take action."

No matter how you slice it, copywriting uses words to connect any goods, services, or products with customers.

The words a copywriter creates form the core foundation for advertising and marketing. But, I assert that copywriting does so much more because copy also educates and persuades.

Without copywriting, ads and marketing would rely on images to convey meaning. Talk about a guessing game. You'd need amazing artists and photographers to move the needle without the use of words. While a picture does say a thousand words, using the right words makes connecting with customers much easier.

Using words correctly will bring to life messages about anything—especially products and services that offer solutions to problems.

1

WHEN DID COPYWRITING
BECOME A "THING?"

While the concept or definition of copywriting might be new to you, words have been used to reveal and influence since the beginning of time. John 1:1 says: "In the beginning was the Word, and the Word was with God, and the Word was God."

If you take Wikipedia's definition of copywriting at face value, then copy written in the Book of Genesis between 1400–1450 BC is logically an example. Since many—like me—view the Bible as a Divine product and The Ultimate How-To Guide, we also view the first book contained in it (Genesis) as the oldest form of copywriting.

If copywriting educates and persuades, then the story between Eve and the serpent in the Garden of Eden demonstrates both concepts well. Stick with me, and I'll show you how.

Remember how the serpent stresses the benefits Eve will receive when she eats the forbidden fruit? Of course, he did that through deception while pinging on her wants and desires. Satan even includes a little:

- Fear of missing out (FOMO),
- Reciprocity (do this, and you'll get that), and

- Justification factor (it sounds reasonable, so it must be true*).*

Sadly, this biblical story showcases negative uses of techniques countless people use in their copywriting today.

From the Garden of Eden to Modern-Day Ads

Years later, early history shows that using printed words to sell things involved the arduous task of writing everything by hand. Producing advertisements for circulation meant copying ads over and over again. (Talk about a painstaking endeavor.)

Johannes Gutenberg invented the movable type printing press around 1440, which transferred ink to paper mechanically and accelerated the printing process.

Research shows one early ad was a handbill selling printer William Caxton's prayer book around 1476 or 1477.

By the early 1600s, weekly newspapers started appearing on street corners throughout Europe. The increasing popularity of weekly publications found publishers carrying advertisements to offset printing and distribution costs.

From the beginning of time until now, the art of copywriting has evolved into a critical component used in every aspect of communication and marketing today.

2

EXAMPLES FROM
YEARS GONE BY

Much is written about professional copywriters like John E. Powers and Claude Hopkins, who earned a living writing in the 1890s. Each of them established copywriting standards, some of which are still used in some form today.

John Powers—who insisted on writing truth when honesty wasn't a popular industry trend—wrote ads that were direct and told the literal truth. For example, when someone asked Powers to write an ad to get rid of a store's surplus of gauze-like fabrics called "rotten gossamers," he wrote:

> *"We have a lot of rotten gossamers and things we want to get rid of."*

By telling the truth, the store sold out by noon on the day the ad ran.

When Powers wrote this copy for neckties, they flew off the shelves so fast the store couldn't meet the demand:

> *"They're not as good as they look, but they're good enough—25 cents."*

Fast forward to 1957, when Clairol became a household name with the launch of their first at-home hair coloring product using this ad copy:

"Does she…or doesn't she? Only her hairdresser knows for sure."

Within six years of this product launch, seventy percent of women were coloring their hair at home! These few examples show how the writer knew what would get customers to buy. Translation: Knowing your audience well will help you use the right words to get prospects to take action.

Words Permeate Everything

Copy doesn't just live in advertisements. How do we know this to be true? Because we use words that sell, educate, and persuade in nearly everything we write and speak.

Consider, for example, a Kickstarter company that launched their first product called Baron Fig, which later became their company name, back in 2013. While they sell writing tools and notebooks, they harnessed the use of good copywriting to connect with their audience.

The company's "Our Story" (or About) page[1] begins with these sentences:

> *We make tools for thinkers.**
>
> **If you have thoughts, you're a thinker.*
>
> *Five things you should know about Baron Fig. Hey, who doesn't love a list? Here are a few things that you should know.*

The J. Peterman Catalog[2] is another example that showcases the use of emotions to connect with customers. (While you may remember hearing about the J. Peterman Catalog from the *Seinfeld* show that aired from 1989 to 1998, the *real* J. Peterman Company began in 1987.)

---

[1] "Baronfig - Our Story." Accessed April 5, 2022. www.baronfig.com/our-story

[2] "J. Peterman Company Catalog." The J. Peterman Company. Accessed April 5, 2022. https://jpeterman.com/.

Their writing style about the clothing products they sell is real, authentic, and based on stories about how wearing the clothing will make you feel. Here's what they wrote about their first product:

The J. Peterman Duster.

Classic horseman's duster protects you, your rump, your saddle and your legs down to the ankles. Because it's cut very long to do the job, it's unintentionally very flattering. With or without a horse. Although I live in horse country, I wear this coat for other reasons. Because they don't make Duesenbergs anymore.

(In case you're inquisitive like me, you'll appreciate knowing that a *Duesenberg* was a high-end luxury automobile produced between 1913 and 1933.)

From selling widgets to writing descriptions that help readers experience what you're describing, copywriting is the primary vehicle used to convey messages both on and offline in many different ways. It is fair to say that marketing doesn't exist without copywriting.

3

HOW IS COPY USED TODAY?

As I've worked with entrepreneurs and business owners over the years, many ask, "What qualifies as copy, and how is it used?"

Every time I hear this line of questioning, I respond with, "I'm so glad you asked." Why? Because knowing how and where copy is used will deepen your understanding of how you can use it, too.

In the coming chapters, we'll peel back the layers and look at the various ways copy is used in today's world, as well as Scriptures that address what Christ-followers should do.

It shouldn't be surprising to learn that the Bible has a lot to say about words that sell, persuade, and educate. Look at it this way. From beginning to end, God's Word:

- Sells the benefits of worshiping and walking with Him.

- Shows understanding of problems we experience and offers a solution for addressing each issue.

- Offers business cases that show why we need to consider building a personal relationship with Jesus.

- Persuades us by showing what life is like when you partner with God and when you don't.

- Educates about the best ways to think, speak, and act in alignment with His teachings.

Some messages are shared with conviction and power that go deeper than mere words through the Holy Spirit (1 Thessalonians 1:5a) while other words are used to stir up love and encouragement (Hebrews 10:24).

Sadly, some copy is crafted carefully to serve personal interests by using flattering words, hype, and manipulation to deceive naive people (Romans 16:18b). Like me, you've probably encountered this concept more times than you'd like to remember.

No matter how you look at it, people have been writing and speaking words to peddle wares, instruct and inform, and influence since the beginning of time. Many have done so without realizing they were using copywriting.

From where I sit, I believe that everything written online or printed uses a form of copywriting. Why? Because people use words to convey messages.

Consider that even as a casual Facebook, Twitter, or Instagram user, you are writing copy. But please know this: Just because you've written a social media post online does not make you a professional copywriter. If that were the case, standing in a garage would make you a car, or going to church would make you a Christ-follower.

The long list of copywriting examples includes social posts, ads, blogs, web pages, emails, sales pages, brochures, news reports, magazine articles, and speeches. While some professionals may balk at my viewpoint about what constitutes copy, the reality is that words used to get people to do something—even just liking a post—involve copywriting.

Copywriting—when used correctly—pulls a common thread from beginning to end with the goal of encouraging readers to take action.

PART I
REFLECTION QUESTIONS

Before diving into Part II, consider your answers to the following questions. Write out your responses in your journal so that you can refer back to them.

Points to Ponder

Do you actively communicate with your customers and prospects? If yes, in what ways?

Think about how the serpent twisted the truth for Eve in the Garden of Eden. Have you ever been deceived by marketing copy? What happened, and how did it make you feel once you figured out what happened to you?

John Powers insisted on writing truth when honesty wasn't a popular trend. How is honesty in marketing viewed by many today?

What can you use the Bible to help you do when it comes to marketing and copywriting?

PART II: DEFINING
JOYFUL COPY

4

WHAT MAKES COPY JOYFUL?

While the remainder of this book will dive into why you need joyful copy and help you determine what to write, distill that information, and deliver joyful copy, it is essential to understand the foundation on which *Joyful Copy* stands. Rooted in Galatians 5:22–23 and Philippians 4:8, *Joyful Copy* uses the characteristics found in these verses as a guide. I propose that every aspect of a Christ-follower's life and business should strive to imitate the attributes these verses offer.

As I prayed about the best way to unpack this aspect of *Joyful Copy*, Abba Father reminded me of my pastor's message that compared humans to fruit-bearing trees. Our similarity lies in that humans become like what we focus on and consume.

Think about the structure of trees with me for a minute. Trees that grow tall and strong do so because they are deeply rooted in healthy soil and well-positioned to receive light. The deeper a tree's root structure goes, it will stand solid no matter what happens in the world around it. When a storm comes along, well-rooted trees with strong trunks remain intact while they ebb and flow with the elements around them. Similarly, the tree trunk provides a stable support system for the growth of healthy branches, leaves, flowers, and fruit. While the roots and trunk provide a base anchor, the nutrients from the soil are what give life and create the flowers that turn into fruit.

Over time, trees growing in fertile ground with good nutrients will produce sweet fruit. A tree will flourish with the right food, water, and light. Alternatively, trees that stand in poor soil and out of the light will grow bitter-tasting fruit. When a tree struggles to receive the proper nourishment and water, the fruit may start to rot and eventually die off.

Similarly, humans who focus on all the negative in the world tend to be insecure, anxiety-filled, walking train wrecks. They go through life with a scowl on their faces like the sky will fall at any minute. According to their worldview, everything is terrible, and they are quick to tell you about it, e.g., how people have done them wrong, all their health issues, and what others did that they didn't like. Whenever the slightest thing goes sideways or inconveniences them, they crumble. Their self-imposed devastation finds them looking for solace in their favorite vices, e.g., chronic shopping, sports, alcohol, or (name your weakness here). Their fruit is bitter, smelly, and a bit rotten.

Alternatively, Christ-followers who deeply root themselves in God's Word, feed off the nutrients found in Scripture, and consistently seek a personal relationship with God are easy to spot because they may have a spring in their step and an optimistic outlook on the world around them. They constantly have kind things to say to others and strive to model sound wisdom and discernment. They don't have to announce what they believe for you to see Christ-like characteristics that showcase love, joy, peace, patience, kindness, goodness, faithfulness, gentleness, and self-control. Their fruit is sweet and savory at the same time.

Don't get me wrong. Every tree and human will experience strife and turmoil at some point. But those who have the right foundation will be better off in the long run. (Jesus gives a similar parable in Matthew

7:24-27 that shows the outcome of houses built on sand versus solid rock.)

Now, let's make a real-life application. Pause to think about the last time you communicated with someone in person or virtually. What type of fruit did you give and receive during your interaction? Was it sweet or bitter? Was it authentic or fake? Did you experience gentleness, or was there a bit of abrasive defiance? The list of good and bad characteristics we are all prone to display is long. These attributes are also very telling because what you see and experience when interacting with others demonstrates what is happening inside the person. What happens in a person's heart is heavily influenced by their focus (or the type of soil in which they are planted).

[PRO TIP] No matter who you are or what you do, whatever you focus on is what will influence how you think, communicate, and act.

Thankfully, God's Word (aka The Ultimate How-To Guide) recommends a laundry list of traits for God's children to think about, imitate, and share. Ideally, those same attributes will also show up in the words we write in our marketing and copywriting.

With a goal of better understanding, let's look at the character traits found in Galatians 5:22–23 before we look at ways to determine, distill, and deliver joyful copy. The following sections will focus on the specific biblical attributes: love, joy, peace, patience, kindness, goodness, faithfulness, gentleness, and self-control.

5

(PURE) LOVE

We can love because He showed us love first.
—1 John 4:19, Joy's Paraphrase

*Love is patient, kind, and thoughtful. Love
never shows envy or pride. It does not
brag and is not arrogant.*
—1 Corinthians 13:4, Joy's Paraphrase

Love is a complex concept that most of us desire and search for our entire lives in one fashion or another. The problem is many of us define love in ways that run contrary to what God designed for His children.

Once we understand how the world uses love to get people to do things and God's heart on the topic, we can intentionally show love to others in all we create, write, think, say, and do. This chapter will give an overview of both the world and God's viewpoint on love while offering insights on how you can use love joyfully in everything. (It is clear that an entire book could dive into the topic of love, so I'm hopeful this "taste" will suffice for now.)

Demonstrate Love? Let Me Count the Ways (or Yes, Please)

Man has written much about love and the various ways it shows up in society. But love is also the greatest commandment in the Bible. In Matthew 22:36–39, Jesus shares that each one of us should love God with all our heart, mind, and soul. Following close behind, He says we should love everyone as we love ourselves. (That second one is sometimes easier said than done. Right?!)

Merriam-Webster defines love as "unselfish, loyal and benevolent; concern for the good of another."

Based on those few references alone, it is clear that love is a big deal. So, if love is such a big deal, why does it seem like most marketing and copywriting focus on fear instead? In fact, anxiety is one of the most popular sell-tactics used in today's marketplace.

Don't believe me? Google phrases like "use fear to sell" or "how many people use fear to sell," and 400 to 600 million options will appear. Thankfully, several results seem to focus on the "ethical way to do it."

One headline from *Inc.* magazine reads: "How to Effectively Sell Through Fear Without Going Too Far." (Sounds a little manipulative, don't you think?) The fact is that a constant drumbeat of fear appears everywhere—on the news, on social media, in emails, etc. Sometimes fear is shoved in our faces without apology. Others use the scare tactic of fear (not love) more subtly.

Fear wields great power because it repels us and draws us in. WHY? Because it puts roots deep in the psyche that causes people to freeze, cower, and not get things done. Fear can cause people to take action and buy something, whether they need it or not. (Haven't you experienced some of these reactions yourself?! I know I have.)

Does using fear to get others to do something make you uncomfortable? It does me, too.

The other day, a Done-WITH-You coaching client spent ten to fifteen minutes of our call describing her anxiety about writing some content we were planning for a lead magnet and email series. (We'd already drafted the flow for each piece, so she had nothing to fear. It was just a mindset she needed to overcome.)

As she talked about her fears, several acronyms came to mind:

- False Emotions Appearing Real
- Face Everything and Rise

While we unpacked each concept, an acronym for love surfaced to balance our conversation: **LOVE = L**iving **O**ur **V**alues **E**veryday. Our discussion comparing fear with love was rich and deep; it equipped her to move forward to overcome her fear by keeping her eyes focused on love.

The good news is that none of us entered this world with a spirit of fear because we were all created with a spirit of love, power, and self-control (2 Timothy 1:7). News flash: Fear is a learned behavior. For example, you aren't born afraid of snakes or spiders. Someone teaches you to fear them.

Sadly, many entrepreneurs leverage your anxieties to get you to do whatever they want by weaving it into their marketing and copywriting. In fact, one of the easiest psychological "tricks" to get someone to click buy is by pushing on what they fear.

Fear comes in many shapes and sizes. It could be the fear of missing out (FOMO), fear of the unknown, fear of health problems (e.g., death, infection, gaining weight), etc. The options for fear-based selling are numerous.

Are these techniques effective and memorable? Absolutely. Why? Because fear is a basic human emotion that emphasizes negative consequences.

Since fear works like magic, many marketers and copywriters wield fear as a mighty sword to attract attention and get people to take action. They will pull on the thread of fake fear just hard enough to evoke curiosity, be relatable, and keep people off balance. A quick search of most email inboxes finds subject lines that say things like:

- "Relinquish your fear..."
- "Doubts and fears haunt us all..."
- "Writing without fear..."
- "How to eliminate fear..."
- "YOUR fear of failing not to get…"
- "Before fear gets in the way of…"
- "How to tell your fear to get lost…"

While every business owner needs to understand and address their customers' fear, some people intentionally use that knowledge to manipulate customers to take unnecessary action. (Talk about more smarmy used car salesman tactics.)

How to Persuade with Love

What if you flipped the fear script by using love throughout your marketing, copywriting, and mindset? Instead of pulling on the threads of fear, anger, shame, guilt, or selfishness, why not connect with customers by offering a choice between positive transformation and keeping the status quo. Yes, both fear and love are emotional motivators that cause people to take action. But fear leverages worry and stress while love energizes and supports. Which option sounds better to you?

Your choice seems pretty clear if you're a Christ-following, values-based entrepreneur. When you use love to persuade, the words you say and write will:

- Recognize and acknowledge the fears your clients battle.
- Show compassion and understanding.
- Offer solutions that help solve their problems.
- Give free tips that encourage and inspire.

Remember: fear punishes while love liberates. As you write joyful copy for your business, you will want to pull on the thread of love and use fear only when it is authentic, genuine, and real.

6

(HEARTFELT) JOY

You'll experience joy when you give an
appropriate answer at the right time.
—Proverbs 15:23, Joy's Paraphrase

Pain and sadness are only temporary because God's
abiding joy will transform you after you've
walked through sorrow.
—Psalm 30:5, Joy's Paraphrase

These days, it seems joy occurs in occasional euphoric outbursts that are fleeting. Doesn't it?! That is because many in society convey joy with inflated enthusiasm to generate excitement in others. This brings to mind Oprah standing in front of her live audience enthusiastically shouting, "you win a new XYZ-widget, and you win one, too!" to everyone within earshot. The crowd roars in response, and she keeps up the fevered pitch by adding more and more giveaways into the mix. If you're in Oprah's audience at that moment, you may not have felt joy before she started giving things away, but you are sure to get sucked into the joy train whether you want to or not.

Sadly, this type of joy leaves many feeling empty and flat after the rush is gone. Like a coke that has gone flat, the desire and urge to consume the beverage quickly fades once the fizz disappears.

Thankfully, there is a way to experience authentic joy consistently – even when you may not be feeling it inside. This type of joy only exists when you get it from the Source of all creation. Let's take a moment to look at this fruit of the Spirit and how we can use it in life and business.

Need Your Business to Stand Out? Show Joy.

While joy is not a commandment in the Bible, it is definitely a spiritual discipline and attribute that God asks His children to demonstrate consistently. Merriam-Webster defines joy as a "source or cause of great happiness." But, M-W also defines joy as "success in doing, finding, or getting something; to experience great pleasure or delight."

Biblical joy is dependent on who Jesus is and not what is happening around us. Godly joy comes from Holy Spirit guiding us in all we think, say, and do each day. Deep abiding joy will come only from remaining in God's presence and focusing on the hope and promises in His Word.

So how can you weave the concept of joy into what you write, say, and market about your business? It is hard enough to get attention from customers and prospects because of everything vying for attention. (Right?!)

Short of setting your hair on fire while standing on your head and flailing your arms around, it may seem easier to replicate what most "gurus" tell you to do in your business? I understand the frustration because I've been there, too.

Here's what I know to be true: If you want to stand out in today's noisy marketplace, the last thing you want to do is look like everyone else.

You're probably thinking, "But, Joy, that is easier said than done." And you are right because taking a stand to be different is challenging. But there's a secret I learned as a little girl that I know will help you achieve results. (Stick with me for a minute.)

This tip may sound crazy, but I promise it DOES work. Are you ready for your "new" insight to help you stand out?

Put yourself last.

It may sound shocking. But if you put yourself last, you WILL stand out.

Since we live in a me-focused society where most people put themselves before anything else, especially if you live in the U.S., one of the easiest ways to get noticed is by focusing on others before yourself.

Why? Because it's NOT about YOU. It's about THEM. What I'm describing is both a copywriting technique and a biblical principle. (See Matthew 6:33 and Philippians 2:3–4.)

Renowned agnostic Robert Ingersoll said it well in the 1800s: "We rise by lifting others." The bottom line is that helping others will drive your success because giving pays off in oh-so-many ways. The key is doing for others without expecting anything in return. The "fruit" you'll start giving out is nothing but authentic joy when you practice this approach. Remember M-W's definition of joy: "success in doing, finding, or getting something; to experience great pleasure or delight." Putting yourself last while sincerely and authentically doing for others (in a right and balanced way) will produce joy.

Three Easy Ways to Practice Joy

I want to give you three easy ways to use joy in your life and business. The first example came from my mom. Her approach is to help others without expectations. She does this by complimenting everyone she encounters—even strangers. I know that may sound odd, but it is part of her DNA and something she learned from her father.

When Mom passes out joy, she's instantly memorable and has more friends than she or I can count. But when you spread joy, make sure you do it with sincerity because most people can tell when your joy and encouraging words are fake. In Mom's case, she has an added bonus because she has cultivated a list of friends—new and old —with whom she can easily connect and on whom she can depend because her focus has been on them.

A second easy way to remember to use joy is through an acronym I learned as a young child that also uses my name. Perhaps you know it already. Regardless, I know it will help you, too. The acronym for JOY = Jesus first, others second, and yourself last. (Pssst, putting yourself last is also a key to long-lasting happiness and success.) When you consistently apply the JOY acronym to everything in life and business, you will also start to view the world differently.

[PRO TIP] Those who focus on their customers before themselves achieve results. Think about it for a second. People typically don't visit your website or online storefront because they like you or what you do. Don't get me wrong. Being a nice person and offering problem-solving solutions is part of the success equation. Prospective clients seek out your business because of the transformation your solutions bring to whatever problem or pain they are experiencing.

So, in each interaction, make sure you weave in joy. Why? Because only pulling on the thread of negativity, despair, and sorrow does not demonstrate the godly attributes God calls Christ-followers to show. No one wants to be around a Debbie-downer.

Are you wondering how you'll apply this concept to what you write about your business?

[PRO TIP] Don't write about yourself. You'll experience results when you apply JOY to all you do. (No pun intended.) Follow these guidelines when you write.

- Use your customers' language to spotlight **their** problems and the possibilities they desire.

- Turn up the volume by showing you understand what's on **their** minds.

- Then suggest the amazing, transformative solutions you offer.

- Weave in authentic, heartfelt joy dependent on a relationship with Jesus.

A third way to practice joy comes by showcasing God's goodness. Help prospects find ways to discover hidden blessings by turning the problems your business solves on their side. WHY? Because every hurdle or problem also generates advantages buried beneath the surface. If you stay focused on the pain and difficulty without looking on the other side, you fail to uncover what God wants to use to help you grow.

Think about it for a minute. Before you created your products or services, didn't you struggle, too? But God used the situations you walked through to help you realize a lesson or gap. The more you analyzed the issue and asked for His help, the more He helped you see the solution for moving forward. When you turn problems on their side, they become growth opportunities that help you experience genuine joy. Use every issue you or your customers encounter to focus on blessings in disguise. Approaching obstacles that way will push you forward into what is next.

This concept is nothing new because James 1:2 spells it out plainly. Count every challenge as joy. When you look at difficulties that way, you'll start seeing what God wants you to accomplish despite the circumstances.

[PRO TIP] When you write about your customers' problems and challenges that you know how to solve, point to the benefits they might be overlooking. Remember, features tell, but benefits sell. So make sure every single stumbling block you point out shines the light on the beneficial blessings they will experience. When you consider the challenges as blessings from God, you'll develop joy for what He is doing in the situation.

7

(DEEP, ABIDING) PEACE

Lift each other with encouraging, peaceful words.
In turn, God's peace and love are with you.
—Corinthians 13:11, Joy's Paraphrase

Turn everything over to God in prayer. His peace that
is hard for most to understand will protect
your heart and mind when you do.
—Philippians 4:6–7, Joy's Paraphrase

These days, peace seems like a fictitious concept as current-day wars, protests, and digital unrest find people beating their chests about one cause or another. Chaotic discourses have become so loud and distracting that it is sometimes hard to hear that still small voice in your Spirit.

Some use the lack of peace as a weapon in their toolbox to get people riled up and agitated. They secretly love playing the antagonist or poking the bear to get reactions. Some marketers, politicians, business owners, activists, and even some who speak from pulpits use the peace versus conflict buttons to gain support for their cause, evoke change in specific directions, and (gasp) line their own pockets.

It is important to be aware of the various ways people stir the pot ever so subtly. But it also means you and I have a choice to make about how we show up in life and today's marketplace. Are we going to promote peace in all we do, or will we leverage conflict to get our way?

Are You Promoting Peace or Conflict?

Everywhere we look today, battles are easy to find. You don't have to go looking for conflict because it will find you whether you want it or not. Pick almost any topic, and opposing opinions emerge from nowhere as others tell you why that concept is bad, wrong, or harmful. Conflict, like fear, is divisive and causes people to do what they normally wouldn't do.

On the other hand, peace seems to be a hard commodity to locate. According to Merriam-Webster, peace is the "freedom from disquieting or oppressive thoughts or emotions; harmony in personal relations." Just reading the definition seems to evoke soothing feelings in today's conflict-filled world, doesn't it?

To illustrate the point, the fable of Henny Penny comes to mind because it demonstrates how easily conflict can get people lathered up. Did you ever hear the story of Henny Penny when you were growing up? If not, here's my quick synopsis.

One day Henny Penny kept getting whacked on the head by acorns as she picked up corn in the yard. Since she didn't know how or why this was happening, she thought it meant the sky was falling. Alarmed by this self-imposed revelation, Henny Penny set off to tell the king. Along the way, she started collecting a rather large following of critters who heard—and bought into—her tainted version of reality. In turn, they began to believe that the world was coming to an end. It's easy to imagine a growing mob meandering down the road chanting, "The sky is falling!" As the moral of the story starts to emerge, the group encounters Foxy Loxy, who decides to trick everyone into taking a shortcut to get to the king's palace. Sadly, the easily duped group winds up being eaten by the fox.

Unfortunately, Henny Penny's story sounds similar to how many entrepreneurs, business owners, and influencers operate today. Using a mix of creativity and nefarious plots, many are skilled at stirring the pot with sensationalized stories that create twisted realities to make it hard to distinguish fact from fiction. The concept of peace never emerges as fear, anxiety, and conflict take center stage. Like Henny Penny, the anxiety-laced stories many marketers share are so believable that people are distracted by what is really going on behind the scenes.

But what if Henny Penny had flipped the script and acted cool as a cucumber? Do you think she would have created a mob-like following of critters who were quickly whipped up into hysteria? Probably not. If she had handled the situation calmly and peacefully, what do you think would have happened? Would there even be a story to tell? Maybe, but it wouldn't be filled with chaos.

Offer Peace Instead of Discord

As entrepreneurs and business owners, you choose how your brand and reputation show up in the marketplace. You may create an anxiety-filled environment where clients walk on eggshells and wait for the other shoe to drop. Perhaps you take it a step further and get your audience to focus on pie-in-the-sky wealth obtained by pursuing the pipe dreams you sell. Or you may choose to build a world filled with God's love, radiating peace and showcasing leadership.

[PRO TIP] Values-based entrepreneurs will make every effort to pass out peace no matter what is happening in the world around them (Philippians 4:6–7). Sometimes it is easier said than done. Right?!

Follow the steps below to elevate the peace your products and services bring.

- Write out the benefits of your solutions without weaving in nefarious, sensationalized tales.

- Write five to ten different ways your solutions demonstrate each of the following peaceful characteristics:
    - Success
    - Fulfillment
    - Harmony
    - Security
    - Well-being
    - Freedom
    - Value

- Write how and why your solutions deliver each trait.

- Review what you wrote.

- Pick the best ones.

- Weave them throughout your marketing.

Strive to build a business that doesn't change with the circumstances like Henny Penny's worldview did. Be intentional not to let the slippery slope of conflict stir up your prospects simply to get them to do what you want.

8

(SINCERE) PATIENCE

Don't grow tired of doing good because
you'll produce results if you don't give up.
—Galatians 6:9, Joy's Paraphrase

Does it ever feel like you're consistently playing the "hurry up and wait game?" Me, too! So much so that I am intentional in checking myself and making sure I respond with love instead of annoyance when the waiting game happens.

For example, I'm married to a retired Navy nuc who sets every clock in our house five-ten minutes fast. (No kidding.) I've grown accustomed to it now. But when we first got married, he didn't tell me the "clock secret," so I couldn't understand why everyone else was always "late" to our meetings and get-togethers. (Funny guy!)

It is no surprise that patience is a muscle every Christ-follower needs to exercise regularly in life and business. But a word to the wise, don't pray for God to give you patience unless you're ready to be tested because He will put you in situations where you get the opportunity to practice.

Buy Now Before We Run Out!

We live in a society of immediacy. In fact, we've been conditioned (in the U.S.) to expect everything fast. If we don't get it right now, it is common for whining, grumbling, and complaining to start. Agitation, frustration, and impatience are all emotions we've been trained to display whenever we have to wait. Most marketers know that, so they use immediacy, urgency, and impatience to their advantage.

This concept brings to mind a bit I once heard a comedian share called "Everything's amazing, and nobody's happy." While his well-timed and colorful delivery evokes laughter, his stand-up bit is sadly valid and on point. He describes how things that used to take a long time now happen within seconds (typically) due to innovations. Instead of making people happy, today's naturally occurring delays tend to upset people. It is typical to hear many people respond, "What do you mean I can't have it now?!" followed by gestures and sounds of exasperation.

While agitation, immediacy, and impatience have become accepted norms (in the U.S.), it is not how followers of Christ are to behave. Instead, God calls us to demonstrate patience. Merriam-Webster defines patience as "the ability to wait for a long time without becoming annoyed or upset." As you navigate life, are you showing others patience or frustration through your words and actions?

Do any of these scenarios sound familiar?

- A tailgating car zooms around the vehicles in front of it, only to arrive at the stoplight at the same time as everyone else.

- For the umpteenth time, a voice from the backseat asks, "Are we there yet?" during the first hour of a twelve-hour road trip.

- An ad guarantees "how to lose weight fast without dieting" or "three simple steps for quick weight loss."

- A "guru" promises you'll get results RIGHT NOW when you buy their product.

- Another pledges to share how to "4X your income" or offers a "5X formula."

No Waiting, Instant, Immediate, Now, Get-Rich-Quick, Limited-Time, and more have become like neon signs that flash to capture the attention of anyone who'll listen. It is no secret that the world around us is constantly racing to make everything urgent. So it only makes sense to sell your products the same way. Right?! Actually, that's not right if you want to build an authentic business with sincere working relationships.

When someone raises their hand to work with me one-on-one, I intentionally ask about their desired goals, deadlines, and results. Why? Because I know that success doesn't happen overnight. The right results will come with hard work, realistic expectations, and God's guidance over time.

[PRO TIP] If you want to achieve long-lasting results in your business, you need to practice a balance between urgency and patience in every piece of marketing and copywriting.

Entrepreneur Ralph S. Marston, Jr. describes the process well: "Success requires both urgency and patience. Be urgent about making the effort and patient about seeing the results."

If you're driven like me, you may find that combining patience and urgency creates a confusing conundrum. This quandary reminds me of a grade school science experiment where students are tasked with growing a plant from a seed. Some kids take things seriously by researching what to do and taking time to apply their newfound knowledge thoughtfully by dispensing just the right amount of water, fertilizer, and soil. They take time to nurture their seed so it will grow big, healthy, and strong.

Other students race through the exercise as fast as possible just to get it done. Then they wonder why their plant doesn't produce results and pop up out of the soil overnight. The students who took their time experienced a positive payoff when the time was right. The ones who were impatient and raced through the exercise ended up frustrated and angry. Similarly, many entrepreneurs expect to throw something up and see their cash register ring. But it doesn't work that way.

Those who exercise patience and commit to the long haul in whatever they do know that results take time. Said another way: Keep fighting the good fight even when others around you are racing ahead, looking for quick results and get-rich-quick schemes. Take a stand for your faith in God in public. Don't hide it or try not to offend others by speaking the truth (1 Timothy 6:12). Don't get tired of doing things decently and in order because you'll see results when the time is right (Galatians 6:9).

If you race through your audience and product research, you won't see the same results as someone who methodically walks through the process. Writing about your business to connect with your audience requires patience and self-discipline. Translation: Writing in alignment with the teachings of God's Word might require you to take an extra step or invest more time than you planned. But the payoff is worth it, especially when others realize you're shining God's Light in today's dark world.

Here's What **Not** to Do:

- Don't fall into the trap of instant, get-rich-quick schemes.
- Don't create unnecessary urgency for your customers either.
- Don't tout "limited time" offers with fake scarcity just to make a quick sale.
- Don't stretch the truth or make bloated promises just to close a deal.

- Don't push the sale to anyone who is breathing or has money.
- Don't pressure people into buying.

Be Sure to **Do** These Things:

- Do take time to methodically research and understand your audience.
- Do listen to customers' problems, needs, wants, and desires.
- Do uncover your customers' objections and address them up-front.
- Do develop rapport with the **right** clients you know you can help.
- Do offer valuable insights without expecting anything in return.
- Do focus on patience by consistently showing up and realizing that God will bring you the right clients in His time, not yours.

Remember: When you do the work in partnership with Holy Spirit, results will happen when the time is right.

9

(AUTHENTIC) KINDNESS

Don't share any corrupt or manipulative
thoughts. Only share what will help,
encourage, and benefit others.
—Ephesians 4:29, Joy's Paraphrase

Have you noticed how authentic kindness seems elusive these days? Everyone seems in a rush to get somewhere or achieve their personal agenda. When that happens, many people miss out on opportunities to be kind by holding a door open, complimenting a stranger, or (gasp) by being thoughtful without expecting anything in return.

Entrepreneurs, marketers, and business owners may be among the worst when it comes to dishing out genuine, heartfelt kindness because we tend to focus on meeting goals and getting quick results.

Imagine what would happen if each of us slowed down enough to dole out good deeds to those we encounter along the way? Would the world instantly be a better place? Probably not, but the impact of those random acts will undoubtedly create a ripple effect that lifts up and encourages others in positive ways.

How You Can Master My Most Valuable Skill

"I made this video for you."

"I have a welcome gift for you. Please give me a call."

"FREE CLASS: How to Become a Highly Paid (XYZ)"

"Would you like me to do (XYZ) for free personally?"

Those headlines and snippets of copy sound good, don't they?! These must be sincerely nice people to volunteer information about how to become proficient as a (insert expertise here). Or offer li'l ol' me a gift. The kindness of each item alone evokes curiosity, makes you sit up a little straighter, lean in a little further, and put your reading glasses on to hear what they promise to give you. Right?!

But in some cases—nay, a significant portion of cases—kindness is an illusion used to open doors and wallets. Merriam-Webster defines kindness as an adjective of "sympathetic or helpful nature." But kindness is tricky because many use it as a tool to ingratiate themselves with people. If they offer tremendous value, people will be more prone to do whatever they ask in the future. They offer "valuable" services in an effort to employ reciprocity as a tool to manipulate others to feel the need to reciprocate.

That concept, in and of itself, is not actually bad. Jesus taught us to treat others as we want them to treat us. So, at face value, offering someone something helpful for free that may—or may not—open the door for them to buy from you down the road isn't all that bad, is it? No. I touch on this typical marketing practice throughout this book. But problems arise when we use kindness to manipulate people into repaying "favors."

One example that I've seen repeatedly in copywriting uses kindness in this manner. The sales copy says something like, "You'll find our convo so astonishingly valuable, or I'll pay you $KKKK...." The ad continues with statements like: "What I'll give you is so amazing that I offer it to only a few people who meet these criteria." The copy then lists criteria that just happen to be an exact fit for YOU, the reader. Imagine that!? By this time, you're not only sitting on the edge of your seat because of the uncanny fit and generously kind offer, but you've pulled your phone and wallet closer in case you need to use one or the other to take them up on this generous offer. (Sure enough, the next step does involve you providing something.) Depending on the specific offer, it may be as simple as an email address. Or it could be a deposit to show you're serious about committing to show up and take advantage of their special and kind offer.

Please hear me loud and clear: if you are a Christ-follower and decide to use a similar offer of kindness and generosity *without manipulation or hype*—more power to you. But be **very** careful because marketing like that is a slippery slope easily filled with selfishness and thoughtlessness. That's why I felt led to title this section (Authentic) Kindness.

You see, many people out there display kindness. But they do so with the wrong motives. What they dangle as a carrot of kindness is neither authentic nor honest. Authentic kindness is filled with genuine truths. It isn't copied, false, or artificial. It isn't the type of kindness that someone made up just to get someone to do something. A quick look at Merriam-Webster shows similar definitions.

We need to strive to demonstrate kindness the way God did. Time and time again, Jesus demonstrated authentic and genuine kindness. When He healed the leper, He didn't ask for a deposit to make sure the leper would show up for the healing session. When Jesus fed the hungry, taught people, cared for widows, and defended children, He was showing genuine kindness to the unsuspecting without hidden strings attached. He wasn't secretly hoping that those individuals would remember Him one day and buy something from Him. He was sincerely being kind because He knew He could positively impact and change the lives of those He served. So, He never asked for anything in return for His kindness.

A real example from my own life happened not long ago when someone I respected reached out and offered to meet with me regularly. She knew I could use her help and support to create something God put on my heart. So, she took a stand, reached out, and gave me the support I needed. What struck me was this person never asked for anything in return. She consistently showed up to answer my questions and point me in the right direction. And do you know what? I'll never forget that selfless act because it positively impacted me in so many ways. (I didn't use her name because I'm sure she doesn't want a deluge of people asking for that same kind of support. She did what God put on her heart. But I know when she reads this section, she'll know I'm talking about her.)

Another example happened with my email list not that long ago. I wanted to know what topics kept people up at night regarding copywriting. Since the best way to discover that is by asking your audience, I did just that. To give a little incentive, I offered the first three people to respond to my query a free, no-strings-attached strategy/coaching call. Imagine my surprise when one of the people who received the call boldly asked me to go ahead and give her my pitch. I asked, "What pitch?" And she quickly shared, "Surely you have a pitch—something you want to sell me—because I took up your time." It gave me great pleasure to share with her that there was no pitch; I just offered the incentive out of kindness.

Here's the truth: If God calls us to display genuine kindness in our copywriting and marketing, we must be sure that we don't have a manipulative motive behind our words and actions. Show kindness whenever possible, so it works from the inside out to others. That means we need to show compassion to those who don't deserve it. (That last one is sometimes the hardest thing for me. But it is how Jesus acted, so we should, too. He even treated those who nailed Him to the cross and persecuted Him with kindness.) If you look up the antonyms for kindness, you'll see words like harsh, ill-will, indecency, selfishness, and thoughtlessness. The call to action for Christ-followers is straightforward and simple: In whatever copy you write and marketing you execute, display authentic kindness backed by ethical, non-manipulative behavior.

10

(PURE) GOODNESS

*Do things that will promote spiritual
well-being and bring blessing to other believers.*
—Galatians 6:10, Joy's Paraphrase

*For the result of partnering with God
generates goodness, righteousness, and truth.*
—Ephesians 5:9, Joy's Paraphrase

No matter who we are or what we do, we all begin each day with 1,440 minutes to use as we choose. From the moment our feet hit the ground, we subconsciously mirror the negatives or positives we hear and see in the action of others, reported news stories, social media posts, etc.

When things don't turn out as planned, we each make instant choices on how to respond. Free will finds us choosing between grumbling, complaining, and whining, or looking for the bright spot even in difficult situations. Ideally, Christ-followers should decide to make the world a brighter place by seeking out goodness, noticing positives in the smallest of things, and being intentional to see blessings when others do not.

Since human nature delivers a constant drumbeat of discouraging thoughts, the only way to look different and showcase authentic, spirit-filled goodness is for God to help us moment-by-moment, day-by-day.

Goodness May Not Be What You Think It Is

When I determined to understand goodness and how it might apply to *Joyful Copy*, I quickly uncovered a new-to-me perspective hiding in plain sight. All these years, I thought goodness as a fruit of the Spirit was…well, about being good. But research, prayer, and seeking the Lord opened my eyes to a much deeper concept than that.

I discovered that the terms "good" and "goodness" appear over 600 times in the Bible. That fact alone made me sit up a little straighter and lean in to learn more because goodness must be an important concept if mentioned that many times. Right?!

So, I took a moment to look at a few definitions. Merriam-Webster defines "goodness" as "the state of being good." But that definition seemed shallow, which required digging a little deeper. In comparison, M-W defined "good" as "someone who has favorable character."

Just for comparison, I tapped into two more common resources: The Oxford Dictionary and a thesaurus. I found Oxford's definition to be more meaningful and on point as it defines "goodness" as "the quality of being morally good or virtuous." The thesaurus brought more clarity with several synonyms, including character, honesty, integrity, morality, and virtue. Antonyms included corruption and dishonesty.

But the most interesting discovery revealed that God is the epitome of goodness. He is the standard by which we determine goodness. Since humans are made by God and God is good, it is easy to see how humans cannot display goodness the way God does without His help.

Being good is one thing. But having a spirit of goodness flows from Holy Spirit and God's presence working in and through our lives. In essence, displaying goodness is motivated by our desire to act more like God. And we do that by striving to embody the fruits of the Spirit.

Biblical research pointed to several stories that illustrate goodness displayed by humans with God's presence in their lives. In particular, the story of Esther shows her choosing to stand up for what is right and risking her life to protect God's people rather than ignore the possible destruction of the Jews to keep herself safe. (See Esther 4.) And the story of the Good Samaritan found in Luke 10:25–37 found one man taking a beaten stranger to an inn where he paid for his care. What makes this story stand out is that they were enemies by race. Jews and Samaritans did not interact for any reason. Yet, the Samaritan showed the Jew goodness.

In both stories, the display of God's goodness working in and through the main characters' lives is evident and strong. They weren't just good people performing a benevolent act or random acts of kindness, as we like to call them today. They were taking action based upon the guidance of God's presence living in their lives. Today, we call that presence Holy Spirit.

In essence, for you and me to display pure, godly goodness through our lives, businesses, marketing, words, actions, and deeds, we need to rely on Holy Spirit to guide and direct us. People might see goodness in our actions and words, but our hearts must be pure if we are to demonstrate the goodness of Christ in our lives every day.

Let Goodness Shine Through Your Copy

So, how does this apply to writing joyful copy for your business? It is a bit easier than you might think. Let's compare what you write about your business to an apple. An apple is a good fruit that offers many wonderful benefits once you consume it. But if the apple gets dirty, you—or your customers—wouldn't want to eat the apple until it is washed.

Similarly, the apple (writing about your business) makes it easy to showcase the goodness of your products and solutions. But if you spend all your time thinking about ways to get people to take action fast or twisting reality to manipulate people to buy things they don't need, it is like putting mud on your apple (what you've written about your business). The right customers won't want your solutions if you cover them in twisted reality created with your words. Sure, a few will overlook the mud created by your twisted lies and keep moving forward. But the vast majority of the right customers you could be serving will go somewhere else.

To display God's pure goodness through what you write about your business, you have no choice but to invite Holy Spirit into what you're doing. Simply ask God to renew you by filling you with Holy Spirit every day. And ask Holy Spirit to help you hear His voice in all you think, say, and do—and then take action on it. Take it a step further and ask Holy Spirit to help you display pure goodness through all aspects of your business, particularly what you write about your business.

Since the opposite of goodness is corruption and dishonesty, you will want to make sure whatever you write does not display any of those negative characteristics. Write with sincerity and honesty. Let your integrity and God-like character shine through brightly.

Specific copywriting techniques you may want to consider using to display your goodness without calling it that include these below.

1. **Be honest.** Point out your solution's flaws. (Seriously!) Let your truthfulness shine through with facts and examples. Being honest will increase your credibility and draw the right people into what you have to say.

2. **Teach something.** Learning something new will create emotional engagement with your audience, even if it is just a unique perspective.

3. **Tell stories.** Well-written short stories will connect with your audience's mind and emotions more effectively than academic or sales speak ever could.

Highlight your strengths, show confidence, and build trust with heartfelt honesty and Spirit-led goodness. You will display pure goodness in your marketing and copywriting when you do these things well.

11

(RELIABLE) FAITHFULNESS

Jesus never moves or changes. He remains the same at
any point in time—yesterday, today, and tomorrow.
—Hebrews 13:8, Joy's Paraphrase

My passion hobby finds me diving into the depths of the ocean to marvel at God's beautiful creations that few get to see. Since none of us were born with gills or fins, breathing underwater requires special equipment and training that helps us play underwater tourist.

From my training to my dive gear to my consistent dive buddies (Robert and Sandy), they each need one critical element: reliability. If one of those elements is out of whack and proves not to be faithful, a life-or-death situation could quickly arise.

That is why I am selective about what gear I buy and who I let service it. My training never ends as I try to learn something new each time I dive, instead of thinking I've arrived or know it all. Most importantly, I only dive with those I trust with my life because if something goes wrong, I want to know they have my back.

Faithfulness in those things is critical if you want to dive into the depths safely. Similarly, God's faithfulness shows up in life in many different ways. Let's take a moment to unpack this fruit of the Spirit and how we can apply it in life and business.

Take Faithfulness to a Different Level

The world we live in turns the concept of faithfulness on its head because we live in a society of fair-weather friends, wavering political parties, varying ideals, fluctuating beliefs, and shifting ideas. What we get behind and wholeheartedly support one day can change on a dime if someone presents enough information to make us switch over. Sometimes we don't even need compelling facts to change our relationships, products, or vendors.

Writing those last sentences made me think about cell phone carriers and customer loyalty. Some of us have been with the same cell phone provider for decades and would never dream of switching, like me with my four-decade journey with Verizon. Others are always on the lookout for the next best deal or offer. Given the right incentives, some people will hop from vendor to vendor, chasing promos and giveaways.

This same scenario plays out with various businesses that we all use in our lives. From cable and Wi-Fi providers to physicians to restaurant chains, some stick with the same everything while others enjoy the hunt and thrill of the chase. When we lived in Charleston, the end of every contract provided a new opportunity to see which cable carrier would give us the best deal. It was interesting that the cable providers knew this game existed, and if you said the right words to them, they would magically give you a sweet deal to stay.

Sadly, many view relationships the same way. Have you noticed how long-term personal and business relationships don't happen as they used to when our parents were growing up? Working at a company for life was a "thing" generations ago. But today, hopping from one place to the next is the norm. Even marriages with vows that say "for better or worse" don't really mean staying together through thick and thin, do they?

It is much easier to live out our world's version of faithfulness with a short-term, easy-out back door that gives us each the option to change our mind at any time. And the excuses we come up with for making these pivots and swings are rich and self-serving. Most of the reasons have a root cause of not meeting our needs in one way or another. But no matter how we try to justify it, genuine faithfulness in today's society is rare and hard to find.

Ironically, God has a lot to say about faithfulness, as He mentions it over eighty-five times in the various translations of the New Testament alone. We'll unpack that in a moment, but let's dive into the definitions first.

According to Merriam-Webster, faithfulness means "true to the facts, loyal, and full of faith." Cambridge defines it as "trusted, firm, unchanging principles." With those thoughts in mind, the antonyms are easy to connect with fraudulent, dishonest, careless, and unscrupulous at the top of the list.

But God's Word views faithfulness differently than most of us do. In fact, the Bible speaks of faithfulness in four ways:

1. **Faithfulness is an attribute of God.** Think about that for a moment. One of God's main characteristics is faithfulness. He embodies it. He IS faithful. Hebrews 13:8 spells it out plainly by saying that Jesus is the same yesterday, today, and tomorrow.

2. **Faithfulness is a positive human characteristic.** The two people that come to mind who displayed faithfulness well over their lives are my parents. They were always faithful to God,

each other, and me. Pause to think about anyone you have known who consistently displayed faithfulness in their lives. Then pray for God to bless them.

3. **Faithfulness is a characteristic most of us lack.** While I could wax poetic and list examples of faithless people, I'd prefer to ask you to reflect on your own life. Don't spend too much time on it. But who has let you down for one reason or another? Once you have your list, pray for each person and forgive them for what they did.

4. **Faithfulness is a gift of the Holy Spirit.** Galatians 5:22 lists faithfulness as a fruit of the Spirit, but it takes intentional action to possess and embody those characteristics. I believe this to mean that when we invite Holy Spirit into our lives, He works in and through us to help us display godly faithfulness in our lives.

As an essential part of who He is, God's faithfulness is reliable, unwavering, and steadfast. He doesn't have to work at being faithful because it is part of His makeup. However, as humans, we have to make a daily, conscious effort to seek the Lord, meditate on His Word, and follow His guidance for faithfulness and the other fruits of the Spirit to grow and mature in us.

Faithfulness doesn't come to us instantly. You don't perform or do faithfulness. It is cultivated from the inside out. It is a daily discipline that shows up in our lives by being diligent over time.

The good news is God does call us to make the spiritual fruit. Our job, as Christ-followers, is to plant, water, and cultivate spiritual fruit in our lives and through our businesses.

We do that by not being swayed by the pressures others put on us to make decisions, take actions, or produce changes. This means that faithful, Christ-following entrepreneurs will never seek to cut corners, cheat others, or act unjustly.

The Bible is filled with multiple passages showing faithfulness demonstrated in big and small ways, from well-known patriarchs like Moses to unfamiliar characters like Silas, Tychicus, Epaphras, and Onesimus.

Five Ways to Showcase Faithfulness in Your Work and Life

- **Be Reliable and Unwavering.** Let everything you think, say, and do be consistent. Avoid the shiny object syndrome that finds you flitting from one thing to the next. Let your friends, family, prospects, and customers know they can count on you no matter what. Don't be a "here today, gone tomorrow" person. Ask the Lord to help you remain steadfast in alignment with Him. He will not let you down.

- **Be Committed.** Stop giving excuses and start delivering on promises. While it is tempting to make last-minute changes, remain firm and unchanging. Unless God directs you to go in a different direction, stay the course and follow the game plan you created in concert with Him. Make thoughtful decisions and keep your commitments. Let every commitment begin with Him. Your Spirit-led faithfulness will become a beacon of light others rely on when you do.

- **Be Disciplined.** Easier said than done, but those who create habits see success. If your goal is to let God's light shine brightly through your writing, you need to create a discipline to invite Him into everything you do. Don't create something and then ask God to bless it. Start with God. Ask Him for direction and guidance, and He will be faithful to give it to you. Make this process a part of how you navigate life and business as well as what you write. You are guaranteed to start showing up differently.

- **Be Humble.** Keep your focus on your audience by showing genuine understanding. Admit your mistakes and weaknesses. Be transparent and show your raw underbelly that most people typically hide. Don't strive for perfection. Eliminate self-aggrandizing copy that spotlights your awesomeness. Arrogance and cockiness will block your ability to show God-given confidence and Spirit-filled faithfulness.

- **Be Relational.** Jesus' life and ministry did not lead with the Gospel. He didn't go out and start preaching to everyone He met. He was intentional in cultivating genuine and authentic relationships. His actions showcased hope and love. He didn't say things just to get people to do something. He didn't pressure people into doing what He wanted them to do. He consistently and faithfully nurtured relationships over time. Likewise, we should do the same with our friends, family, and prospective customers.

12

(SUPERNATURAL) GENTLENESS

Gentle words melt anger while careless
words stir the pot.
—Proverbs 15:1, Joy's Paraphrase

Words of encouragement give life, but words
that twist reality condemn and bring harm.
—Proverbs 15:4, Joy's Paraphrase

At face value, Merriam Webster defines gentleness as a "mild character trait or temperament." Similarly, Oxford defines it as "softness of action or effect."

When I read those definitions, I hear subliminal undertones of weakness. It makes me think of the interactions between George McFly and Biff in the Back to the Future series. Time and again, Biff finds ways to verbally abuse and embarrass mild-mannered George McFly, who always seems to cave in to whatever Biff wants to say or do.

Thankfully, the biblical definition of gentleness is much different and better. Baker's *Evangelical Dictionary of Biblical Theory* states that gentleness is "sensitivity of disposition and kindness of behavior, founded on strength and prompted by love."

Before I share my ah-ha moment, let's look at some of the antonyms for gentleness. The list of opposites is quite long and includes behaviors we commonly see in society today, such as irritability, harshness, gruffness, audaciousness, indifference, presumptuousness, aloofness, and unkindness.

Take a few seconds to reflect on the behavior we see happening in the world around us today. People reflect those negative attributes more than ever. Our observations should make us more intentional about showing godly gentleness in everything.

Apply Liberal Amounts of "Holy Duct Tape" As Needed

As I continued to study this concept, I came to a new realization. Gentleness is interwoven with all the other spiritual characteristics we are called to display in our lives. Think about it for a moment. You're not harsh, gruff, or indifferent when you show joy. You express joy with an undercurrent of gentleness. The same applies to the other fruits of the Spirit: love, joy, peace, patience, kindness, goodness, faithfulness, and self-control are all lived out with a current of gentleness running through them.

While gentleness is inseparable from the other traits, you will fully display it only with Holy Spirit living in and working through you. If you try to be gentle on your own, you'll only get so far. It is something we have to seek out and do every single day with Holy Spirit's help.

I like to say that I've applied "holy duct tape" when I start to say something and feel Abba clamp His hand over my mouth before the words come out. Sometimes the core message of my thought is good, so I feel a prompting to revise my words, so they reflect the Lord.

We don't have to go far to find examples of the best ways to weave gentleness into our thoughts, actions, and words because Jesus demonstrated it continually. Do you remember that time He showed gentleness to the adulterer the Pharisees brought to Him in John 8:1–11? Instead of reacting legalistically, He told those without sins to throw the first stone at her. Once all the accusers walked away, He gently told her that He didn't condemn her either and to go live a life without sin.

What I find even more interesting is that Jesus never did anything for personal gain. Everything He did was intentional to bring glory to God. And He did not do it from the sidelines. He hung out with drunks, thieves, and angry people. He intentionally put Himself in the midst of the mess we call life to shine God's light brightly. Sure, doing so brought out the best critics who tried to mock Him and punch holes in His way of living, but it never worked.

Gentleness comes from humility. Look at it this way: the opposite of gentleness finds people self-aggrandizing and putting themselves on center stage. All they do is talk about themselves, how awesome they are, and how they are the best thing since sliced bread. Don't believe them? Just ask them. Sadly that is what we're taught to do for success as entrepreneurs. The mantra is to sell yourself and what you do for others. Be aware that this approach may be displayed with all types of humility, making it essential to discern and look beneath the surface. Why? Because anyone can fake humility while having a heart full of arrogance and pride.

[PRO TIP] What if, as a Christ-follower, you flipped the script and showed your understanding of others and the challenges they are walking through in life and business? When the time is right, you could sell how what you sell will help them navigate those hurdles. See how gentleness and humility shine through with this practical application?

Genuine humility starts in the heart and generates gentleness that you display to others. Ego isn't involved. Gentle humility takes you off center stage and helps you influence others through the lens, strength, and power of Holy Spirit.

I'm hopeful that you're starting to view gentleness differently than before. If so, you may be wondering how you can display gentleness in the words you say and write about your business. In addition to the pro tip shared earlier, consider trying these few steps:

- Start by putting God and others first. (Remember JOY = Jesus first, Others second, Yourself last)

- Live with less judgment and more compassion.

- Avoid speaking harsh or condemning words to others.

- Demonstrate gentle strength and self-control.

- Apply Holy Spirit-led holy duct tape as needed. (If you need to borrow some, I'm willing to share. I have "holy duct tape" by the truckloads.)

- Take yourself off the pedestal. Never assert your superiority, awesomeness, and self-righteousness.

- Be helpful and kind to others even when they have wronged you.

- Eliminate the water torture marketing techniques that browbeat people into buying what you're selling.

Remember, gentleness is a characteristic that shapes and colors everything you do. The fruits of the Spirit aren't imperative commands that you generate with your effort. Spiritual fruits result from partnering with the Lord in **all** you do. *Joyful Copy* works the same way. When you get closer to Jesus, you will experience His gentleness. In turn, His gentleness will shine through you and what you say, create, and write to others.

13

(GODLY) SELF-CONTROL

Partner with God in everything you do (in life and business), and He will help you produce results you never imagined possible.
—Proverbs 16:3, Joy's Paraphrase

Most of us plan what we're going to do, do it, and then ask God to bless it. But He's waiting for us to let go and partner with Him.
—Proverbs 16:9, Joy's Paraphrase

On a surface level, those two verses (Proverbs 16:3 and 9) talk about planning with God. But if you look deeper, you'll see these verses are actually talking about exercising self-control and partnering with God in everything.

But what appears in the Bible and how society uses it seem disconnected. Have you noticed how the concept of self-control seems surreal in a world where most people embrace the ready-fire-aim mentality? Interestingly enough, everyone is born with the power to exercise self-control. Whether we use it or not is another thing.

Sometimes we apply self-control in one area of our lives but throw caution to the wind in other situations. Sure, approaching life with wild, free abandon is fun. But there are always consequences for doing so. Most of the time, letting down your hair without applying liberal amounts of self-control generates bad results.

Is Self-Control an Oxymoron?

Maybe self-control is an oxymoron because there is evidence of people acting without thinking everywhere we look. These days it seems that controlling one's emotions and actions is elusive. I'm guessing you've seen similar poor choices like these:

- Customers who loudly share their exasperation because they feel the line is moving too slowly.

- Food addicts who use sweet treats as a crutch to soothe the pain or angst they're experiencing.

- Chronic manipulators who smugly justify using twisted words to sell things or get people to do something.

- War news showcasing the ravings of a power-hungry man who will crush anyone or anything that gets in his way.

- Defiant alcoholics who insist on having a drink regardless of the consequences.

- Entrepreneurs who make grandiose promises to get people to buy XYZ (vaporware) products that, ultimately, leave people disappointed.

- Shopaholics who buy things they don't need on impulse.

- (Describe person) who (insert behavior) to meet their (insert desire).

Many of us sit back in awe as the erratic and rash behaviors of others are broadcast on the news, displayed online, or happen around us. At the same time, some sit on the sidelines "eating popcorn" while they egg them on and applaud their poor choices.

Whenever things go sideways, most people give excuses saying they didn't realize what would happen or never considered the consequences of their actions. Most find ways to justify their behavior and make whatever occurred seem okay. But close examination makes it easy to see that acting with wild abandon or in self-serving ways always results in repercussions and scars. The bottom line: A lack of self-control will always end with someone being hurt.

Let Your "Yes" Mean Yes and Your "No" Mean No

Our mission as Christ-followers, should we accept it, is to start practicing self-control and let our "yes" mean yes and our "no" mean no. In our business, marketing, actions, words, and deeds, self-control should be more than a figure of speech.

Most know how to define self-control, but many struggle to possess it. Though countless people talk about self-control and strive to achieve it, the enigma is that few come close to having it because they give in to their needs, wants, and desires by acting on impulse.

Let's pause for a moment to look at the definition. Merriam Webster defines self-control as "restraint exercised over one's own impulses, emotions, or desires." Cambridge dictionary states self-control is "the ability to control your emotions and actions."

It is easily defined and explained but challenging to exercise. After watching human behavior for a while, I wonder if self-control is so elusive that no one will ever achieve it. Thankfully, the short answer is no, as history has shown many who held back when they could have wreaked havoc.

A quick look at the synonyms for self-control is very telling. Words like balance, constraint, stability, self-discipline, and willpower speak volumes. These words also bring to mind many examples—from others' lives, my life, and perhaps even your own—when people have refrained from scratching that itch to act on a whim and do what felt good at the moment.

Call it whatever you like, but a lack of self-control resembles anger, agitation, bullheadedness, greed, headstrongness, impatience, instability, and willfulness. And these are just a few of the antonyms that describe one who is not controlling their actions.

It seems logical to think that self-control has become obsolete. Since most find it difficult to achieve, maybe its "time" was meant for years long ago. *Right?!* Wrong. If you look around, you see that many use self-control to achieve their desired state of being or goals. Bodybuilders come to mind as an example. Those rock-hard bodies don't magically appear by living a life on impulse. Cut muscles are built over time by hard work and discipline.

While we all don't desire to be bodybuilders, as Christ-followers, we strive to look, think, and act like Jesus. To achieve that requires putting our desires and impulses aside while we put Abba in the driver's seat.

It is intentional that the Bible talks about self-control a lot. Abba knew how our human nature would get in the way, so He equipped us well. In fact, 174 verses in the Old and New Testaments (NKJV) mention self-control. At its core, biblical self-control involves choosing to let go and let God.

Think about that for a moment. When you've made plans for your business or written copy to market your wares, did you do it first and **then** ask God to bless it? We're all guilty of that childlike behavior at one time or another. But doing it that way is missing out on the opportunity to invite God in from the beginning and partner with Him.

Giving up control of things, people, situations, and actions isn't easy. Our human nature finds most of us wanting to be in charge. We like to force things to go our way. So it is no wonder that when things don't work out, we whine, thrash, complain, and get upset.

Here's the Good News

When we realize we have the option to turn control of things, people, situations, and actions over to God–and we let go and let God be in charge of every aspect of our world–that is when transformation happens.

Choosing to work in partnership with God instead of controlling the outcome ourselves sounds like a lofty ideal that someone invented. It sounds surreal and unrealistic. Doesn't it?!

I mean, why would the Creator of the Universe have time for or even be concerned about what is on our minds?! He's got better things to do than listen, guide, and direct us every step of our way throughout every day. *Right?!* Wrong.

He created us in His image, not someone else's. HIS image. Why? Because He wants us to worship Him and do life in partnership and relationship with Him. When we seek to apply Christ-like self-control that is only available by aligning with God, He will help our minds, emotions, outward actions, and internal beings become more like Him.

Before we consider several simple ways to use self-control in marketing and copywriting, let me offer you some steps for partnering with God every day.

- Before you do anything, thank Him for what He has done in your life. Be specific and list that for which you are grateful.

- Invite Holy Spirit into your day by asking Him to help you hear His voice in all you think, say, do, and create.

- Ask the Father specific questions about what He would have you do. Then listen for His response and take action on them.

You will learn to hear what He says if you do this regularly. Sometimes you might be surprised, but most of the time, He will fill you to over-flowing as He lovingly and gently takes you where He wants you to go.

By submitting to God and allowing Him to partner with you in every-thing, you will be exhibiting self-control because you've exchanged your free will for His will. It is a choice you must make. He will never force you. So, what choice will you make moment by moment, day by day?

More Proactive Steps to Take

Since we find the lack of self-control woven into the books we read, movies we watch, and commercials that want to sell us solutions for the problems we've created, Christ-followers have a golden oppor-tunity to stand out and look different.

The "you do you" mentality embraces the lack of self-control and re-wards people for impulsive living. "So what if doing XYZ will result in ABC (horrible) outcomes. If it makes you feel good, DO IT!"

This mindset has become so commonplace that keen observers have found a way to capitalize on it. Indeed, many people are happy to get rich off of the instability of others.

If You Have This Itch, We Have An Easy-To-Swallow Pill For You.

High-pressure sales tactics seasoned with manipulative words push the right buttons to get your attention and offer "never-before-seen" ways to help you get what you need... FAST.

Instead, take proactive steps to weave self-control into all you do.

- **Apply liberal amounts of "holy duct tape."** Since we are walking billboards for Christ, we must react and respond in ways that glorify Him. If we respond with sarcasm, harsh words, or crass thoughts, we look no different from those around us. Just because we think it doesn't mean we need to say it. Hold back those thoughts. Exercise self-control.

- **Don't dangle (self-serving) carrots in front of prospects.** Some marketers intentionally make their solutions sound so appealing they create impulse buyers who throw caution to the wind and self-control out the window. Don't use shiny object syndrome to get people to buy something they don't need or won't use. While it works, it is wrong and manipulative. Exercise self-control.

- **Focus on the value your solutions bring others.** Instead of offering hype-filled fantasies and promising instant results just to make a sale, showcase the benefits customers will experience. Highlight what your services and solutions do without making false promises, and the right people will buy at the right time. Don't fabricate benefits and results just because "it sounds good" or everyone else is doing it. Exercise self-control.

- **Stop creating false urgency with fictitious deadlines**. While urgency has been used for decades to sell and close deals, the deadline that gets someone to do something is often contrived and false. In turn, the seller and the buyer leave self-control behind when they both follow their desires. Don't get me wrong; urgency is a great selling technique if the deadline you give is real. Since we know people rush to make decisions when we give them deadlines, Christ-followers are wrong to make a fictitious deadline just to move the needle. You're saying you don't need God's help, guidance, or direction when you do that. Exercise self-control.

Let His Light Shine

While we can share much about the fruits of the Spirit and how to apply them to our lives and businesses, Christian characteristics are rooted in faith, truth, and hope which is found only in a personal relationship with Jesus Christ. When we strive to sincerely partner with Him in all we do, His light is what others will see in our work and lives. If you're a Christ-follower who wants everything you create, write, and share to align with God and His Word, your copy will be joyful.

Before we jump into the following sections of this book, I want to remind you (and myself) about the promise found in 1 Corinthians 13:13. This verse says that during our time on earth, we are to stay focused on the faith, hope, and love God brings. But the greatest of those is love. And the best news is that one day when we go home to be with Jesus, our constant faith and hope will receive the reward of His love for eternity. How beautiful is that?

Consider this for a moment: God calls Christ-followers to infuse the words we write and the solutions we create with God's faith, hope, and love. Our marketing copy should shine the light on all of the fruits of the Spirit, but especially on love.

To make sure your words are joyful, you may want to use the *Joyful Copy* Checklist I created. (See the end of Chapter 20.)

PART II
REFLECTION QUESTIONS

Before diving into Part III, here are some questions to consider. You may want to add your responses to your journal to refer back to them later.

Points to Ponder

What is the foundation for *Joyful Copy*?

What would make your copy not joyful?

If the foundation for *Joyful Copy* extends beyond the words you write for marketing, what else in your sphere of influence should emulate godly characteristics?

Is it possible to know about godly characteristics and not display them in life and business? Write out a few examples of how this might happen.

Divide a piece of paper into two columns. On one side, list all the ways you display godly traits in your life and business. On the other side, list areas you could improve by aligning them with God's Word.

Take a moment to praise God for the areas where you're already displaying godly characteristics. Then ask God to help you with the areas you need to improve. (Hint: Ask God to show you two or three to focus on improving with His help. Then praise Him for what He helped you accomplish. Rinse and repeat.)

PART III: WHY DO YOU NEED *JOYFUL COPY?*

14

"NOW IS THE WINTER OF OUR DISCONTENT"

This famous quote from Shakespeare's Richard III resonates more loudly today than ever: "Now is the winter of our discontent." Everywhere we look, the words people write, speak, and share are creating dividing lines and stirring up angst.

We've entered a time where it is consistently hard to trust what we read or hear to be true or right. What appears to be true may or may not be, making it hard to discern reality from manipulation and hype. Like a cat creeping up on its prey, deceptive thoughts subtly work their way into *everything* we consume—especially in today's online world.

Because it is easy to drown in the deluge of conflicting information and twisted realities, those who want to survive seek guidance. Sadly, seeking outside input trips up many people because they get counsel from the wrong source. But those who lean into godly wisdom and discernment as they navigate life and business learn how to cut through the noise and write ethical copy while holding their head high.

This battle of the mind is nothing new as it has been occurring since Eve listened to the serpent. Similarly, it is easy for what we write for business to influence others joyfully or manipulatively.

Thankfully, several verses address how to write business copy that is authentic, aligned, and joyful. (Hint: I lean into these two verses when I create and write so much that I've memorized them.)

Proverbs 3:5–6 teaches believers to trust in the Lord with **all** (not some) of their hearts. We aren't supposed to compartmentalize God and allow Him to bless only specific things. The Bible teaches us to trust Him with everything. The verses instruct us to trust Him without leaning into what we think we understand and to acknowledge Him in everything. If we do all of that when we write, He **will** direct our paths. That promise alone provides a solid foundation for writing joyful copy.

But Galatians 5:22–23 lets us see that those who lean into Holy Spirit for guidance will also strive to write and market using the fruits of the Spirit. In other words, what we write will authentically showcase love, joy, peace, patience, kindness, goodness, faithfulness, gentleness, and self-control. I didn't see anything to do with manipulation, hype, self-ish ambition, or envy in that passage paraphrase. Did you? Yet much of what we read these days is peppered with the subtle antithesis of the fruits of the Spirit, which validates the need for writing joyful copy.

As you research and plan what to write, you will probably find it easier to copy what some other guru teaches or sells. But instead of copying someone else, why not ask God to help you and show you what to plan and write. James 1:5 tells us that if we don't understand some-thing, we simply need to ask God for His wisdom, and He will give it to us freely. Simply ask Abba Father for guidance. It is that simple.

But I don't believe that request is a one and done. Just like the energy we get from a meal wears off and we need to eat again, the wisdom and guidance we get from Holy Spirit will wear off, too. This example clarifies why I think it is important to ask Holy Spirit to fill us anew with His wisdom and discernment *each day* so we hear His voice in all we think, say, and do. (You will hear this concept and several others repeated throughout the book, which reminds me of the old sales adage that I apply: "Tell them what you're going to tell them. Tell them. Tell them what you told them.")

Let's walk through a true story that will illustrate why joyful copy should be part of the communication toolbox of every Christ-follower.

Please Yourself, Others, or God?

A certain individual had a personal quest to live his life in alignment with the teachings of the Bible. He applied this desire boldly to every aspect of his life.

Some people thought this man's actions were strange because he didn't blur the lines between right and wrong. But he didn't care what they thought because he wasn't living his life to please others or himself. He was living his life to please only God while ensuring no one could ever question his integrity or character. He had an unwavering determination to do what was right according to the teachings of the Bible, no matter what the situation.

Long before koozies or coolers were invented, people used sacks to keep beverages cool. It was not uncommon to receive your bottled or canned soft drink wrapped in a brown paper bag because they kept drinks colder during hot summer days. Not long after brown-bagging sodas became a norm in the U.S., some people started pretending they were drinking soft drinks when they were actually drinking alcohol. It was a sneaky way to get away with drinking booze clandestinely in public.

This subtle transition throughout the U.S. seemed like an innocent change to many. But the reality was that this deception made it hard to know who was drinking a soda or an adult beverage.

Committed to letting God's light shine through him in all he did, this young man decided to eliminate the appearance of evil in all that he did. (1 Thessalonians 5:22 says to throw out anything tainted with evil.) When he made this choice by not drinking soft drinks wrapped in a brown paper bag, some people thought his actions were odd and made fun of him. But everyone knew, without a shadow of a doubt, where his principles and convictions were founded.

Now, don't get me wrong. This young man didn't grandstand and say, "Look at me and what I'm doing." He didn't point his finger at others and say, "You're doing things wrong; follow my example." He simply lived out the teachings of the Bible in every aspect of his life. He became a living example of what it means to align with the Word and let God's light shine to others. He emulated letting his "yes" mean "yes" and his "no" mean "no." (Matthew 5:37 says just that.)

Years later, the young man would share this story with his young daughter (aka me). As Daddy told me what he did and why, I must say I struggled to understand the significance or importance of it. In fact, like many others, I found what he shared to be odd and unusual.

Little did I know that his example would show me how to live my life. Many decades later, what he modeled in this story rang true for me in oh-so-many ways, as I desired to live life in partnership with God. Finally, the proverbial lightbulb went off as I understood the importance of integrity and always doing my best and what is right.

One of my favorite quotes sums it up well: "Integrity is doing the right thing, even when no one is watching." People attribute this quote to many different men, from C.S. Lewis to Coach John Wooden. Regardless of where the quote originated, a Christ-following entrepreneur should weave it into every aspect of life and business.

When the world is filled with confusion and people who twist the truth to meet their own purpose—you have a choice to make. You can choose to look, sound, and act like everyone else. As many like to say, "Everyone's doing it, so it must be okay." Or you can be like my dad, who took a stand to be authentic, genuine, and true in everything he did. Which way will you choose to show up in the world?

You may be wondering what this story has to do with writing. The answer is simple: *everything*. You must choose whether to write about your business authentically or write words that subtly twist reality to get people to take action. In essence, you must choose whether your life and business will please God, others, or yourself.

As everyone around you continues to crank up the volume by using lies, deceit, and distorted truths—you must choose whether your marketing and copywriting will look like everyone else or authentic and aligned with God's Word.

15

THE INTERNET
SHRANK THE WORLD

Today's online world has made the world smaller in oh-so-many ways. Namely, because we can communicate with people around the globe in seconds. The evolution of the Internet has eliminated the boundaries of time, space, or distance. What some described as futuristic in decades past is now a reality.

For many of us, today's reality seems surreal as we think about how it used to be compared to how it is today. Looking back over several decades, it is easy to see sweeping changes in everything from writing papers to connecting with others.

For example, every paper I wrote in college required me to walk, ride, or drive to the library to conduct research manually. In fact, using a computer with a search engine wasn't even an option because it didn't exist.

(To squelch your curiosity, I was born in 1965 and see age as just a number, not an expiration date. Ha! But I digress...)

Way back then, I used a card catalog and the Dewey Decimal System to "surf" the library shelves and find the books that might or might not contain the information I needed. Compared to today, using the index and table of contents took an enormous amount of time. Flipping through pages to hunt for details was tedious. Writing out key points to possibly use in my papers happened methodically over hours, days, and weeks.

If I wanted to connect with someone in a nearby town, state, or country, my only options were to pay for a long-distance call that charged by the minute, send a handwritten letter delivered by mail, or travel via plane, train, or automobile to see that person.

Reflecting on the past and writing these memories out makes me feel my age because those methods now seem archaic. The irony is that I grew up using tools far more advanced than the ones my ancestors used. Perhaps you can relate, too?!

While the power of technology permeates everything we do, today's online world didn't magically arrive on the scene overnight. Timelines show[3] work on Internet prototypes originating in the 1940s, but people didn't commonly use the Internet to connect government, industry, academia, and private parties until the 1970s. By 1994, this tool served 16 million users around the globe, and, as of this writing, over 4.5 billion people[4] access the Internet daily. That translates to 62 percent of the world (and counting) using the Internet to live, work, and play every day.

A side-by-side comparison of life before and after the mainstream adoption of the Internet shows many striking differences. You could probably add a few to the quick snapshot, too.

---

[3] "A Little History of the World Wide Web." Accessed April 5, 2022. https://www.w3.org/History.html.

[4] "Internet World Stats." Accessed April 5, 2022. https://www.internet-worldstats.com/stats.htm.

Before the Internet	After the Internet
Paper Maps	GPS on mobile devices and in vehicles
Physical books, magazines, and newspapers	Digital copies of everything
Time-consuming research using a card catalog	Online research within seconds
Phones tethered to walls and outlets	Palm-sized phones
Long-distance calls charged by the minute	Unlimited calling to anywhere in the nation
Country to country calls that were cost-prohibitive	Face-to-face communication with anyone in the world for FREE or pennies on the dollar
Computers that took up large amounts of space in buildings	Palm-sized computers that fit in our pockets
Socializing with people in person	Socializing with people electronically
Shopping in physical stores	Shopping online with doorstep deliveries by mail and drones
Learning through in-person classes and reading books	Virtual learning and online membership sites
Paper checks and cash	Digital payments online
In-person business meetings	Virtual meetings with people

and conferences	from around the globe
Advertising to the masses on billboards and TV or in printed magazines, newspapers, and paper fliers	Targeted advertising in your web browser or social platform based on your specific interests
Ads you discovered as you moved through the world	Retargeted ads that follow you online based on your online activity

Instant access to information has transformed lives and impacted nearly everyone around the globe in one way or another. Today, anyone with WiFi can access places, people, and businesses anywhere in the world within seconds with the click of a button.

While traveling to meet our needs has become optional, it has also opened the doors to a new marketplace where knowledge and goods are now commodities. Online selling has become commonplace as we receive a constant stream of information and items to buy.

Ironically, as the world has become smaller with instant communication around the globe, human interactions have shifted negatively. Relationships lack the depth and warmth they once had. Many of us are glued to devices that serve information based on our individual interests without the need for personal connection. Sadly, isolation and independent living have become the norm.

Non-Stop Access and Round-the-Clock Selling

The information age has also created opportunities to sell products and services seven days a week, twenty-four hours a day.

Many seem to think that selling to needs, wants, and desires took off with the mainstream use of the Internet. While cyberspace did allow for exponential growth that impacted billions around the globe, using psychology to create desire started shortly after God created man.

In Genesis 2:16, God told Adam he was free to eat from any tree in the garden that He gave them **except** the tree of knowledge of good and evil. God told Adam he would certainly die if he ate from **that** tree. God gave that one simple command before Eve entered the scene and exercised her choice to obey or disobey God. (The concept of free will makes its first appearance in the human psyche with this command.)

Genesis 3 recounts the first time selling focused on needs, wants, and desires happened in the world. It is interesting to note how Satan used words to plant ideas that fed into Eve's needs and wants to create desires (Genesis 3:1-7).

It is easy to see how Adam and Eve didn't need anything. God gave them everything needed to meet all their needs. But Satan used words to make what was off-limits seem appealing and desirable so that Eve would justify breaking God's one command. The evil one convinced her that eating the forbidden fruit was okay.

Before Eve's encounter with Satan, creation didn't operate based on needs, wants, and desires because they had what they needed and lacked nothing. But once Eve gave in to the temptation and disobeyed God, lying, deception, questionable motives, manipulation, and hype entered the world from that day forward.

Fast forward to where we are today. Everyone appears to be caught in an ongoing cycle of lies mixed with truth to the point that it is hard to determine fact from fiction. Sadly, manipulation is commonly accepted in all aspects of life and business today.

16

YOUR THOUGHTS
AND WORDS DO MATTER

Since Eve and Adam took those first bites of the tree of knowledge, good and evil have waged a never-ending war to dominate the minds and hearts of every human on earth. This ongoing battle occurs primarily through our thoughts.

Why do thoughts matter so much? Because whatever or whoever dominates your focus will control what you say and do.

If you reflect on your focus during the pandemic and recent political scenes, you will see the impact the words you ingested during lockdown had on your psyche. As a captive audience with unlimited time to focus on the news and social media, most of us fell victim to the continual stream of polarizing thoughts shared.

Think about everything that sucks up your energy, time, and thoughts as the world is getting back to a new normal. Some things subtly sneak in to steal your focus, while others are more blatant. From scrolling social media to work projects to ruminating on the past—the list of what draws your focus or distracts you is endless. Whether you want them to or not, random thoughts and time-wasting distractions are constantly filling your mind without you realizing how much time has passed.

An online search helped me discover a very telling list of nine insidious distractions that derail many from focusing on what truly matters. Blogger Joshua Becker's list included commonplace time-wasters that keep many of us stuck.

Do you heedlessly spend a good deal of your time on these unproductive thoughts?

- The Promise of Tomorrow
- The Pursuit of Perfection
- The Regret of Yesterday
- The Accumulation of Possessions
- The Desire for Wealth
- The Need for Notoriety
- The Pull of Comparison
- The Appeal of Pleasure
- The Presence of Indifference

Abba Father knew the battle for the mind would become our Achilles' heel from the moment He gave us free will and the choice to obey Him. In fact, God's Word describes the immense power thoughts have over each one of us. Here are two verses I've paraphrased that speak specifically to this concept:

- Proverbs 23:7 says what you focus on and think about is how you'll act.

- Proverbs 4:23 instructs you to be careful how you think because your thoughts shape your life.

Our thoughts and minds are prized possessions that many seek to dominate for their own benefit. Many people use the psychology of words to creep into our heads and take up residence without us even being aware of it.

What Does Your Mindset Have to Do with Copywriting?

By now, you may be wondering what your mental process has to do with copywriting. The short answer? Everything. Stick with me, and I'll connect the dots.

At face value, the term "psychology" seems to have little to do with your thoughts or words. Merriam-Webster (M-W) defines psychology as "the science of mind and behavior or the mental or behavioral characteristics of an individual or group."

The definition alone seems innocuous. But if you look a little deeper into the root of the word, you will gain further understanding. M-W shows that the word "psychology" combines the Greek *psychē* (meaning "breath, principle of life, life, soul") with *logia* (which comes from the Greek *logos*, meaning "speech, word, reason").

The etymology of the word "psychology"[5] reveals that it was considered the study of the soul in the 1650s, the mind in 1748, and modern behavior in the early 1890s. If you let that sink in for a moment, it is easy to see that your mind, thoughts, and actions are intertwined with words, no matter how you slice it.

We see a basic example of the power words possess in an age-old classroom project that many scientists have also conducted; the experiment involves common house plants and music. (Perhaps you did this science experiment as a child like I did, too?!)

---

[5] "Etymology of the Word 'Psychology.'" Online Etymology Dictionary. Accessed April 5, 2022. https://www.etymonline.com/word/psychology.

The experiment found that plants exposed to uplifting classical music grew twenty percent bigger than similar plants without exposure, and those exposed to hard rock music deteriorated quickly and died. If the sounds and words of music can impact plant growth, imagine what words do to the thoughts and actions of humans.

A report from *Psychology Today* dives deep into the impact of negative versus positive words and thoughts on brain waves for both the speaker and the listener. Their study showed that negative or fear-provoking thoughts stimulate internal turmoil, while positive words and thoughts enhance well-being and satisfaction.

On both sides of the proverbial scale, negative and positive thoughts—whether real or not—cause people to act based on how those thoughts make them feel. While most never think about it, many know that the psychology behind words can manipulate what people think, say, and do.

Many recent examples have come to light about news media and political figures using words to twist reality and benefit their stance or position on specific topics. A quick Google search will provide many examples if you'd like to see them.

Now that we've touched on the psychological power of words, let's dive into how psychology works in what people write about products and services.

17

YOU'RE THE MOST IMPORTANT INGREDIENT

Did you know that 80 percent of your buying decisions are emotional, and 20 percent are rational? Since emotions affect actions, many marketers and entrepreneurs—even some who profess to be Christians—use emotions and principles of persuasion to sell you what you don't need.

Let's look at a few examples of emotional selling to demonstrate how copywriters have used persuasion over the years. But you may want to put on your seatbelt before moving forward because some of these examples—while very real—are downright scary because they are so subtle.

In the 1940s, animated cartoons would flash words to plant the seed of what someone wanted watchers to do. A 1943 Daffy Duck film flashed the words "Buy Bonds" for a couple of frames when the United States used bonds to finance the national defense programs. (Even the U.S. government understood and used the power of words to influence behavior.)

In 1957, the words "eat popcorn" or "drink Coca-Cola" were put into frames of movies, which resulted in dramatically increased sales. Subliminal messaging is real and works even to this day.

More recently, one online retailer's ad showed a beautiful lady with a headline that said, "You are the most important ingredient." Their creative use of words and images was intentional to draw in women buyers. How? Because subtly, your brain is primed to think you'll like whatever they sell, especially if you're a woman because YOU are the most important ingredient.

Yes, making connections, building relationships, and selling are facts of life and perfectly normal. But, using emotions to create a false sense of desire or fake need for whatever you're offering is deceptive.

If you're a Christ-following marketer or business owner, you will strive to create genuine connections with your customers' **existing** and **real** needs in mind (Exodus 23:1a, Proverbs 6:16–19). You won't create fake solutions that profess to meet those needs just to get customers to open their wallets.

Sadly, many entrepreneurs, business owners, salesmen, and even politicians use this bait-and-switch trick to move the needle. Getting people to take action, buy something, or cast a vote based on false premises or manipulated information is underhanded. Unfortunately, many think nothing is wrong with doing so.

Since people use psychology to write effective copy that connects with an audience, it is important to understand standard writing techniques and ethical ways to use them. Let's look at the psychology of copywriting from some well-known perspectives.

Only 8 Hours Left To...

You've seen emails or ads before with similar words. "Only 8-Hours

Left to (insert action here)." Have you ever noticed how a limited supply of something makes everyone want it? From the beginning of time, humans have wanted what we couldn't possess.

Urgency, exclusivity, and the fear of missing out (FOMO) are typical marketing and copywriting techniques used by many. They work because everyone wants to belong, and no one wants to be left out or miss out on an opportunity.

Please understand nothing is wrong with making sure someone doesn't miss an opportunity IF the deadline and offer are sincere without hidden agendas and phony realities. What makes these scarcity tactics bad or unethical is when they are used to manipulate someone to take unnecessary action. While it is fine to use urgency in copy, these techniques take a turn when a deadline is fake.

Think about the last time you extended a deadline for something you were selling. Was moving that deadline wrong? Not necessarily. But, if you kept moving your deadline just to increase sales, you may need to check your motives. Were you making an offer with a disingenuous undercurrent and selfish motives? Was that your intent from the beginning? Then you aren't being authentic and truthful with your prospective customers. An easy solution is to stop, ensure your offer is factual, and be straightforward with your customers. They will respect you in the long run.

Exclusivity also becomes twisted when it is clear that the seller planned to let as many people into the program as they could get instead of limiting the numbers as stated. If you set a limit, threshold, or deadline—make sure you stick to it and don't waiver.

Using copy to get prospects to take action is not the problem. But if a person's original intent is laced with manipulation, their true character is lacking.

While many methods exist to get prospects to take action and move people forward, let's touch on some of the more common psychological techniques used in marketing and copywriting today.

Using emotions and persuasion is so popular for selling that you can find massive amounts of information written about the topic. One favorite resource, and the favorite of many marketing professionals, is found in Dr. Robert Cialdini's book *Influence, where* he breaks down what he sees as the key elements of persuasion used consistently today.

We've already touched on the concept of scarcity. Let's touch on the other five of Dr. Cialdini's "Principles of Persuasion" that are commonly used in marketing and copywriting. We'll touch on problems you might encounter as a Christ-follower with each one if you're not careful.

Reciprocity

Various dictionaries define reciprocity as "the notion of giving someone something to engender goodwill and get them to do something in return." Used correctly, this age-old technique isn't wrong. The concept of "I'll scratch your back if you scratch mine" is okay if it is used with good intent and follows the Golden Rule found in Matthew 7:12. Remember? Treat others as you would have them treat you.

A classic reciprocity example is found in the "free" samples given in grocery stores next to the product. Sellers intend for their generosity to evoke reciprocity, making people feel obligated to buy the product because they took a sample. (I bet you're thinking about those things you bought that you didn't really need right now, huh? Yeah, I've been there, too.) Now, please don't misunderstand because not all reciprocity is bad. There is nothing wrong with allowing someone to sample products to help them determine whether or not they want to buy it. Potential problems arise when sellers use reciprocity to manipulate people into repaying "favors."

Business owners cross this fine line when they use "free samples" like bait to intentionally suck someone into a rabbit hole deliberately designed to milk the buyer for as much money as possible while not delivering on promises. The problem occurs when a business leaves an intentionally manipulative reciprocity breadcrumb trail to sell vaporware or offer pipe-dream promises they already know they won't fulfill.

Such practices remind me of a real-life situation where someone used a webinar to intentionally draw in a specific target audience and sell them on an idea "God gave" them. The forum required payment in the form of participants' email addresses and their time to listen. Yes, the online seminar did offer valuable insights that any participant could use. (So far, so good.) But, the end product being sold (for a LOT of money—think four and five digits) was nothing but vaporware with no planned deliverables. As participants felt themselves magically being drawn into the presenter's web, they were signing up for a phone call where they would discuss whether this product was right for them or not. Unfortunately, several people that I personally know were bilked out of their retirement money during that call and never experienced the results promised to them.

The lesson here is to make sure you use reciprocity authentically and genuinely without a hint of deception, embellishment, or twisted reality. Besides, it is important for Christ-followers to sow good, non-self-serving seeds that align with God's Word. Galatians 6:7–9 says that those who do things (in life and business) to please themselves for their own personal gain will earn destruction ultimately. One way to avoid this is by weaving the fruits of the Spirit in everything you think, say, and do (Galatians 5:22–23).

Commitment and Consistency

It's been proven time and again that when someone makes a commitment or investment in something, they are prone to follow through and finish the task. For example, you may decide to charge a small fee for someone to attend your summit or online webinar. Why? Because the concept of having "skin in the game" makes someone more invested. (If you want people to show up, consider charging a small fee as it usually works wonders to achieve your goal.)

Problems arise when people use commitment and consistency to mislead intentionally. For example, some toy manufacturers heavily target children by advertising about ONE specific toy they "need" for Christmas. Many parents find themselves making promises that Santa will get *that* toy. Here's the rub: Historically, toy manufacturers intentionally underproduce *that* particular toy, so parents end up buying it in January and February when the manufacturers and stores need to boost their sales. (Have you been caught in this web? Yeah, me, too.)

The concept of commitment and consistency uses psychology by getting your prospect to make a small commitment and convert them into a customer. The long-term benefit is that your new customer will more easily say yes to larger purchases down the road.

Let's touch on a few other real-life examples that you may have witnessed at some point along the way, too. A typical marketing model finds a business holding a "must-attend" conference by selling tickets for pennies on the dollar. All the individuals have to do is buy the $95 ticket to reserve their seat, book their flight and hotel, and show up. Once the person attends the conference, the event is structured to slowly dangle carrots of opportunity for other products that cost four, five, and six digits. And if they buy "right now" at the "special" conference rate, they will get all these other bonuses that aren't available anywhere else.

This example of taking prospects and clients through a growth funnel is a standard way of operating for many businesses today. While the ascension model concept is not wrong, building on commitment and consistency becomes twisted when sellers lay out a breadcrumb trail of manipulation with empty promises to intentionally bilk as much money as possible from those who listen.

Another example finds a self-proclaimed guru spending a significant amount of time talking about the value of being introspective. This teacher tells the students to reflect and ask themselves specific questions about their life, goals, business, and "the possibilities." The instructor emphatically encourages compliance from everyone to complete the assignment, telling participants they cannot move forward in the apprenticeship program without writing out answers to these questions and turning them in for personal, individualized feedback designed to help each person reach their goals. In this illustration, the commitment comes by moving from passive listening to actively writing out responses. But in this real-life example, problems surface when the instructor gives little to no response in return. The students put more into the assignment than the teacher ever intended to provide.

The examples of commitment and consistency are endless because they happen in today's online world all the time. While nothing is wrong with each situation up front–the hidden intentions, unfulfilled promises, or lackluster results baked in from the beginning are where the situations turn sideways.

If you use commitment and consistency in your marketing strategy and copywriting, make sure you do so with integrity, honesty, and ethics. Colossians 2:8 counsels believers to look out for people who try to use big words and intellectual double-speak to dazzle others. In doing so, your commitment may be used to get you to do things in the future you never imagined or intended to do.

Social Proof

The practice of using endorsements and recommendations for business is nothing new. Today, everyone uses social proof to sell, especially in the booming online marketplace. But social influence goes deeper than testimonials or reviews.

Social proof is rooted in the psychology that most people will follow the actions of the masses. For example, you're more likely to eat at a busy restaurant than at an empty one because you regard the actions of others as proof. Studies show that ninety-five percent of humans will imitate what they see before initiating a new behavior.

Like everything else, social proof becomes slanted when it is used to misrepresent or inflate reality. Sadly, fake social proof is real and is now considered the norm by many. Case in point, you can find how-to guides and articles about how to fake social proof. One article touted "how to fake building credibility when you're a new brand."

One insider's slippery slope example finds colleagues and business owners endorsing and promoting each other's products. Cross-promotion alone is perfectly normal and natural in business. It is common practice to create a contest among your business friends to see who will sell the most products for you. With a behind-the-scenes scoreboard, the winner of the "game" gets financial rewards and bragging rights for stacking up the most sales to their customers.

To make this example clear, let's look at the players and their respective roles.

- The product owner is selling purple widgets that claim to produce XYZ-transformational results.

- Colleagues A, B, and C all agree to send out a flurry of emails and social posts to their business email lists and social media followers, pushing them to buy purple widgets fast.

- Each colleague offers testimonials and endorsements about how awesome the purple widgets are and builds hype around this "must-have, life-changing" widget.

- Every member of the insider's contest pushes their list and followers HARD to buy before XYZ deadline. They even throw in a laundry list of bonus offerings just to sweeten the pot and entice their list and followers to buy.

This "I'll scratch your back, if you scratch mine" contest is commonly used and a regular way of conducting business.

BUT there are hidden facts behind-the-scenes that most never realize. Typically, none of those colleagues have ever used the product. In fact, they have little to no knowledge about whether the purple widgets produce said transformations. The only thing they know is if they sell the most, they will be handsomely rewarded with a cut of each sale.

Participating colleagues become so focused on winning that they will do almost anything to use their email lists and followers as pawns in this game. Some go so far as to ask their team members to buy as many products as possible under different email addresses and aliases just to inflate the contest board stats. Others will make up fake testimonials and endorsements just to make it "sound good" and push people to buy.

Within a week or so, email after email fills inboxes with deceptive, high-pressure tactics designed to get the recipients to believe the fake social proof and take action. In turn, unsuspecting customers who don't realize they are being manipulated are blindly following these pied pipers. "If XYZ person I know, like, and trust says it works, and I need this now, I had better buy it," becomes the common mindset.

Hear me clearly: There is *nothing* wrong with promoting someone else's product if you are sincere in your endorsement and motives. But, the fake social proof becomes devious and dishonest when the person promoting the product has never used it.

Many Scripture verses tell us how to use our social influence correctly. In 1 Thessalonians 2:3 God's Word is clear about asking others to do something without any impure or deceptive motives. Galatians 5:22 spells out the need for Christ-followers to act in love (not selfishness) and patience (without pushing others).

The lesson here is to make sure whatever you present to others as social proof is authentic, genuine, and beyond reproach. And always make sure you're sharing real testimonies—not made-up ones—about whatever you're offering and selling.

Likability

The power to influence others is wrapped up in the concept of likability. The more you like someone, the easier they are to get along with and the more capable of persuading you to do something. When you have something in common with someone, that person can draw you in more easily.

Many people use this by weaving into their website About copy or Bios things they have in common with their prospective customers. You can use this method in any copy to show people you've "walked a mile in their shoes." Nothing is wrong with stating your commonalities, as long as what you share is true and not a figment of your imagination or slightly twisted reality.

Since it doesn't take much to get people to like you, some salespeople intentionally seek out any common ground that will help them connect with customers. They may hone in on similar interests or offer compliments designed to draw someone in for a sale at some point down the road. The key is to make connections authentically and sincerely without nefarious, manipulative motives.

God's Word tells us to make sure whatever we do in life and business is honorable, noble, genuine, trustworthy, and faithful. (See Galatians 5:22–23 and Philippians 4:8.) Sadly, many people intentionally use "phony likability" to get what they want. One example appears to happen over and over again in faith-based communities. Perhaps you've seen it, too. A business owner will pretend to have a personal relationship with the Lord and make very specific statements to pique the interest of Christ-following business owners. Sadly, who that person is when no one is looking doesn't align with who they pretend to be publicly. (I understand this experience all too well because I've been sucked into that web of lies myself.)

With a desire to believe the best of people and follow like-minded leaders, many will buy whatever these individuals sell hook, line, and sinker. They don't realize they are buying information from people who said those things only to draw people into their web. And once you're stuck like a fly, it is hard to break free. So, you end up turning a blind eye to what you see that doesn't align with God's Word. You keep drinking the Kool-Aid the fake persona is selling you.

It is hard in today's world of mixed realities to know who is truthful, honest, and right. The only way to gain clarity is to ask the Lord to give you His supernatural wisdom and discernment so you have eyes to see and ears to hear what is true. I promise if you do ask Him, He **will** answer you. Check out Jeremiah 33:3, James 1:5, and Proverbs 3:5–6.

When you use likability in your marketing and copywriting, be aware that any form of hypocrisy, insincerity, deviousness, dishonesty, or (insert hype here) is wrong; Christ-followers should never use such tactics in business.

Knowing there are wolves in sheep's clothing requires staying alert to ensure you're not getting hoodwinked by a smooth-talking snake charmer, especially when you're considering making a purchase. And, of course, you never want to be the one doing the hoodwinking.

Authority

It's no secret that society respects experts. Many indiscriminately follow someone in a position of power no matter what the authority figure says or does.

Some authority figures command attention simply by their presence. Others only need to wear a uniform, e.g., a doctor's coat, military attire, pilot uniform, first responders gear, to evoke respect. The power of authority works because human nature typically respects *perceived* expertise, status, or power—whether it is real or not.

Sadly, the concept of authority wields such power that many blindly follow figureheads even when those people do something immoral or illegal. Some tend to look the other way or try to explain what the authority person "meant" by their actions or words. In marketing and copywriting, some people elevate themselves with lofty titles and accomplishments to simulate authority they don't possess. Their long game involves helping others climb a proverbial ladder that will open opportunities, garner respect, and cause people to pay inflated prices for their goods and services. No matter how you slice it, manipulation and hype creep in when someone who is not an expert touts expertise.

A real-life example of the psychology of authority plays out on the big screen in "Catch Me If You Can." In this movie, Leonardo DiCaprio recreates Frank Abagnale, Jr.'s life as a master of deception. As a skilled manipulator and innovator, Mr. Abagnale navigated life through eight fictitious identities—among them, an assistant state attorney general, a Pan American airline pilot, a hospital doctor, a sociology professor, and a lawyer—to achieve his own goals. In all instances, he used fake authority and false pretenses to gain the confidence of others and get them to let him do what he wanted to do.

The key for Christ-followers is to use authority authentically with truth and honor (Philippians 4:8, Matthew 28:18). If you're not an expert in something, don't inflate your competency or stretch the truth in an attempt to strengthen your position. Several passages address the concept of imposters and wolves in sheep's clothing who go from bad to worse, deceiving others, including themselves (2 Timothy 3:13, Matthew 7:15).

18

SAY IT ENOUGH, THEY'LL BELIEVE IT

While the Internet and libraries are full of copywriting techniques that work to inform, attract, and sell, covering them all in one book would be overwhelming. So let's look at a few other psychological tactics commonly used to convert skeptics into believers and window-shoppers into buyers.

Repetition = Truth

Believe it or not, repeating something over and over again tends to make people believe what is said. Some call this the Illusory Truth Effect. Why? Because saying the same concept or idea repeatedly makes something familiar and believable.

The more someone hears an idea, the easier it is to accept it as truth, even if it is a lie. Sadly, many salespeople, marketers, newscasters, and politicians know that repetition will make whatever is said more plausible.

Think about those who use their social influence or authority in underhanded ways with fake endorsements or impostor-like credentials. They send out a stream of emails and social posts saying the same thing in different ways. Or they may tout expertise that they've only read about or dreamed of possessing. Similar to the consistent drip of water torture that is used with prisoners of war to get them to share secret information, it is easy to believe anything if you hear it over and over again.

Keep in mind that the Bible instructs Christ-followers not to claim lies as truth or circulate false information (2 John 2:21c, Exodus 23:1a). God's Word also states that we should **not** use meaningless repetition (Matthew 6:7). While this verse talks about prayers being offered like rituals and chants, it also applies to falsely using repetition to convince people that a lie is true. The bottom line is that Christ-followers should *not* create the illusion of truth by repeating something over and over again.

Rhyme-as-a-Reason Effect

A similar approach for building trust is the Rhyme-as-a-Reason Effect. This tactic uses rhyme intentionally because people are more likely to remember, repeat, and believe statements that end with like sounds.

This technique, which many have studied and validated, works well because the rhyme overrides reason and leads to belief. Add in repetition of the rhyming phrase, and people tend to reaffirm the message. The rhyme-as-a-reason effect is used to persuade while influencing people's judgment and decision-making skills.

For example, consider Johnny Cochran's 1995 trial phrase, "If it doesn't fit, you must acquit." His repeated use of this phrase was intentional, and some said he was unconsciously tapping into the minds of the jury to try to subliminally persuade them.

We can find other examples passed down throughout history. For example, what we now say as "an apple a day keeps the doctor away" first originated in 1866 in Wales as "eat an apple on going to bed, and you'll keep the doctor from earning his bread."

The examples below compare two sayings with similar meanings. As you read through them, consider whether you also find the sayings that rhyme to be more memorable and believable.

"What society conceals, alcohol reveals."	"What society conceals, alcohol unmasks."
"Anger restrained is wisdom gained."	"Anger held back is wisdom acquired.
"Drive sober or get stopped by a cop."	"Drive sober or get pulled over."

Just because it is common to use the human psyche against other humans to persuade and manipulate doesn't mean you should do it. The bottom line is that any technique which does not align with biblical principles should not be used by those striving to partner with the Lord in life and business.

While rhyming is an effective way to remember things, it also uses childlike mnemonics to lock ideas into memory banks and make them seem plausible even when they are not. Scripture teaches us to put away childish reasoning when we become adults (1 Corinthians 13:11). Since God gave us the ability to think and reason, it is important to use reasoning skills wisely whenever we market and write about our business or evaluate doing a transaction with someone else.

Because

It may sound strange, but the word "because" motivates most people to do something without giving it a second thought. Research shows that giving someone a reason for doing something typically results in compliance. Using because answers the why question and gives readers compelling benefits for acting. Think back to the earlier example of the self-proclaimed guru who instructed apprentices that they needed to write out the answers to specific introspective questions *because* it would help them achieve their goals and advance to the next stage in the program. The instructor gave reasons why and helped students commit by writing their ideas on paper. He used two psychological motivators together for a power punch.

Studies from the late 1970s have proven the power of "because." (Take a moment to Google "Xerox because" to read about the studies.) When a request is small and followed by "because" together with any reason, most people trust what is said and take action without resistance. If you decide to use the word "because" in your copywriting, make sure you provide genuine reasons why and not made up one ones.

It is important to note that using "because" in your copy to give people reasons and overcome objections is not wrong. But when one consistently peppers their prose with false reasons with hidden agendas that "magically" create unwarranted financial gains or benefits—there is a huge problem needs to be addressed.

Unfortunately, many believers (and even non-believers) emphasize not using manipulation and hype; yet, a review of their work over time shows they have allowed subtle manipulation to take root. Since psychological triggers are a slippery slope, many aren't aware they've strayed off the straight and narrow path. Or they have become so comfortable using subtle words to convince people to act that they feel justified doing it. The "nobody saw, so it is okay" mentality doesn't hold water over time. For example, think about the person who tracks every morsel they eat while dieting. But in private, they secretly eat what they shouldn't because they think no one will know, so it must be okay. After a while, what they have been up to will magically show up in the way they look.

It is impossible to use a little bit of cheating or a little bit of hype and manipulation and think no one will notice. At some point, what you've done and how you're showing up in the marketplace will surface. As it has been said, "be careful that your sins don't find you out" (Numbers 32:23).

The good news is that these concepts are nothing new. In fact, the Bible has a lot to say about most of them. Knowing what is possible makes the quest to write copy that aligns with the Bible even more urgent and compelling.

Hopefully, you can see through the various techniques and examples that a huge opportunity exists to write marketing copy without using underhanded psychological tricks to manipulate customers into taking unnecessary actions. Since many tactics and strategies subtly move people down a slippery path of deception, the need for writing joyful copy—marketing that aligns with Christ-like characteristics—is great. The good news is that God's Word spells out exactly how we should think, speak, and act. And those supporting Scriptures can be used as the foundation and filter for all our marketing and copywriting, too. (You may have noticed that Galatians 5:22–23 and Philippians 4:8 are the core bedrock for *Joyful Copy*. We'll continue to unpack ways you can use these verses throughout the rest of this book.)

Let's wrap up this section about why joyful copy is needed by taking a peek at the headlines and subheadings you see everywhere today.

Made You Click

Headlines are an important part of marketing copy and similar to fishing in oh-so-many-ways. Let's use my avid fisherman husband, Robert, as an example. When he goes fishing, he uses a hook with some bait to lure the fish. If the bait is enticing enough, the fish will bite and get snagged on the hook before being reeled into his boat. Similarly, headlines are used in copy like a hook. If your headline grabs your reader's attention, you stand a good chance of hooking them into scanning and reading more of what you've written.

Today's online world makes the headline important because everyone tends to skim and scan the content on their screens before committing to reading more. In fact, any professional copywriter will tell you that good headlines are critical for drawing in a prospective customer. Headlines are so important that a great deal of information has been written on the topic. In fact, a quick online search about writing headlines found 175 MILLION Google results in .42 seconds and more than 1,000 books about the topic on Amazon.

If you think about it, a headline is the first connection many prospects see from a business. When they come to your website, the headline and subheadings are the first words they see. When they see your ad, brochure, or social post, the headline usually draws the eye first. Headlines are especially prominent when someone is searching online to learn more about a product or service.

It's pretty easy for me to compare Robert's catch and release fishing to today's clickbait headlines. Why? Because sometimes both the fish and people clicking on an ad end up surprised by the results from grabbing that "hook." Some don't realize they are taking on an unexpected journey that will lead them into a fishing well on a boat or onto a sales page to buy something they never knew they needed or wanted. Sometimes the headline-hook is misleading on purpose because it was written with the intent to capture attention, distract, and deceive.

The underhanded marketing technique of clickbait-style headlines grew in popularity between 2014 and 2016, with 19.46 to 25.27 percent of headlines written to evoke curiosity.[6] Clickbait is commonly known as deceptive headlines that prompt readers to click and then don't deliver on promises. In 2020, *Forbes Magazine* reported that the Better Business Bureau warned that sensationalized posts using words like

---

[6] "These Researchers Studied 1.67 Million Clickbait Headlines. What They Found Will Totally Shock You." Inc.com, March 22, 2018. https://www.inc.com/bill-murphy-jr/these-researchers-studied-167-million-clickbait-headlines-what-they-found-will-totally-shock-you.html.

"amaze," "shocking," or "never before seen footage" intentionally take readers to sites that may allow cybercriminals to hijack accounts or steal personal information.[7]

To make sure we're on the same page, here are a few clickbait examples.

- …eliminate $100,000 of debt in less than 90 days…
- …How I earned $475,000 in 30 days and why I will set you up right now to duplicate my success for free…
- …Why (XYZ-type role) Makes LESS than 6-Figures a Year…
- …Earn 7 Figures? Three Things You Must Do…
- …add thousands to your bottom line…
- …open this if you want (XYZ)…
- …3X your rates with this 7-step guide…
- …How I 5Xed my business…
- …the $90K email…

It is easy to see how the money-driven promises entice a reader to click. When you view each of those headlines with a godly lens, it is also easy to see the yellow flag warning that something may be off and probably not aligned.

A few other examples are found in these postcards that came in the mail when we bought our house offer. Notice how they use curiosity and greed to coerce the recipient to take action. They hint at financial rewards or personal gain like a hook with bait trolling in the water.

(By the way, my research revealed that the postcard senders were not representing any legitimate interests except their own.)

---

[7] Suciu, Peter. "From Scams To Mainstream Headlines, Clickbait Is On The Rise." Forbes. Accessed April 5, 2022. https://www.forbes.com/sites/petersuciu/2020/02/10/clickbait-how-baby-yoda-is-mourning-kobe-bryant-and-kirk-douglas-while-giving-up-vaping-and-cbd-to-fight-coronavirus/#1127f6811115.

In today's noisy world, attention-grabbing headlines are not wrong if they intrigue readers without misrepresenting the content behind the statement.

The problem occurs when salacious and outrageous headlines lead to fake news and content that doesn't live up to expectations. When a business manipulates readers with twisted reality or hype that doesn't offer the value promised, it can and will negatively impact a brand, business, or individual.

Businesses use clickbait headlines and psychological triggers in so many ways that it is easy to see how the tactics work to attract attention and get people to take action. Sadly, companies pepper their twisted realities with white lies woven into copy to make false promises sound amazing and encourage people to take action.

Now that we've touched on some of the more popular strategies and techniques used in copywriting and marketing today, we're ready to dive into a different approach that will help you show up in the marketplace authentically. After you work through the reflection questions, join me in the next section to dive into what joyful copy means.

While I've moved quickly to highlight the various ways strategies and tactics to attract attention and convince people to buy, I hope you have a better understanding of the art and science sometimes used by many to tap into the minds and wallets of others. I'm also hopeful you see ways to use these methods ethically and authentically in alignment with God's Word without twisting reality.

In the next sections, we will define joyful copy and dive into steps for writing copy that connects with your customers authentically.

PART III
REFLECTION QUESTIONS

L et me encourage you to dig deep and be transparent with God as you search your heart for answers to the following questions. Write your thoughts out in your journal so you can refer back to your responses over time and see what God has done in and through you.

Points to Ponder

In your business, does your "yes" mean yes and "no" mean no? Or do you sometimes waiver just to please other people?

Are there areas of your marketing that use subtle hype and manipulation? If so, list each area. Then commit to rework every piece of content until it aligns with the teachings of the Bible.

Which of the following distracts you and steals your attention the most?

- The Promise of Tomorrow
- The Pursuit of Perfection
- The Regret of Yesterday
- The Accumulation of Possessions
- The Desire for Wealth
- The Need for Notoriety
- The Pull of Comparison
- The Appeal of Pleasure
- The Presence of Indifference

Give each distraction over to God and ask Him to help you replace it with something He wants you to focus on.

Whenever you've used persuasion tactics, have you used them with good intentions, or did you weave in some subtle manipulation?

- List examples of ethical persuasion tactics you've used in your business.

- Review your marketing and look for areas you need to refine. Once you find them, be intentional to remove any hint of manipulation.

Have you followed someone else's roadmap or purchased someone's cleverness in exchange for the promise of wealth? If you're not sure, ask God to help you uncover anything you overlooked or areas where someone duped you.

Once you discover it, either abandon what you've copied or revise it with God's help by:

- asking Abba to guide you to where He wants you to go.
- listening and taking action on what Holy Spirit reveals to you.

PART IV: *JOYFUL COPY* IS NOT A BLUEPRINT

I t is no secret that effective copywriting is a skill that takes time to cultivate. Master copywriters work hard to perfect their proficiency for writing words that get people to take action—so much so that countless copywriters have created tips, tricks, and techniques that they boast will boost conversions and improve sales.

As a case in point, a quick Google search for "copywriting techniques" pulled up 5.7 million copywriting pointers in .67 seconds, touting blueprints, roadmaps, and courses that will create success and wealth. In this next section, we'll take a look at the blueprints and roadmaps that many snap up like candy in an effort to create success for themselves. We will also look at what God's Word says about copying roadmaps and mirroring those who don't align with His teachings.

Many think that roadmaps and blueprints aren't dangerous. They aren't like cigarettes that can harm others or cause cancer. They are purely innocent tools of business that show someone how to get from point A to point B without making the mistakes others have made. In essence, they are an easy button for creating growth.

Conceptually, roadmaps and blueprints make for sound business advice. But let's dig a little deeper to see if we may be overlooking something. Let's start by reviewing the definitions. Merriam-Webster defines these words this way:

- Roadmap: "a detailed plan to guide progress toward a goal."
- Blueprint: "a detailed plan for how to do something."

While nothing is inherently wrong with either term, how roadmaps and blueprints are used to sell and, in turn, help people focus on the wrong destination is skewed. Sit with that thought for a moment.

Many roadmaps and blueprints are similar to following the pied piper. As the tale goes, the Pied Piper of Hamelin promised to rid the town of an undesirable problem (rats) in exchange for a large sum of money.

Without asking about his methods and eager for results, the town leaders agreed. The Pied Piper then played a pleasant, mesmerizing tune on his flute that caused the mice to follow him to their death. They end up drowning in a nearby body of water. Surprised and dismayed by these actions, the leaders refused to pay. In response, the Pied Piper lured the town children to their end in a similar fashion.

Similarly, many roadmaps today offer to solve a problem for a large sum of money. Instead of music, people use idealist promises and clever words to lure the right target audience. With a hunger to achieve the promised results, many entrepreneurs find themselves paying for plans not written for them to follow in the first place. In turn, entrepreneurs lose money and time when they try to implement the plans yet don't experience what copywriters encouraged them to imagine.

Perhaps you have experienced a similar situation in your lifetime. Maybe you've bought into pie-in-the-sky blueprints and felt defeated when your efforts did not bear fruit.

The reason why so many struggle and fail is because they are not following the plan created specifically for them by their Creator. You see, God has a specific purpose for each of His children, which includes you and me. If you want to live out God's purpose for your life and business, you want to follow the **right** plans by making sure whatever you think, say, and do looks more like your Creator than anything or anyone else. But, you *can't* look like Jesus if you're following the blueprints and roadmaps created by someone other than Jesus.

So, the natural question is, how do you achieve success? How do you show up authentically and ethically in a world where everyone appears to be copying each other? The good news is you already have what you need to achieve success. You just need to know where to look and how to apply the resources in your possession. What if you could follow a *framework* that integrates godly principles with copywriting techniques? *Joyful Copy* will help you do just that.

Before we examine joyful copy more closely, let's pause to examine the word "framework." Merriam-Webster defines a framework as "a basic conceptual structure," which is different from a detailed plan for how to do something. It is important to recognize the difference between a framework and a blueprint. In simple terms, blueprints and roadmaps outline step-by-step best practices created by others to get from point A to point B with promises of specific results. A framework will simply help drive your idea and provide guidance.

By definition and practice, *Joyful Copy* is **not** a blueprint or roadmap. *Joyful Copy* frameworks apply basic copywriting techniques and then seek to emulate Christian characteristics.

Joyful Copy is a phrase I coined when Abba Father helped me see that there is a better way to shine His light in the marketplace. He showed me how writing words to sell, educate, and persuade *does not* require subtle, underhanded techniques.

Extending beyond the basic definitions of the individual words, I use "*Joyful Copy*" and "ethical copy" interchangeably. Both phrases refer to writing copy that aligns with the teachings of the Bible without twisting reality.

Let's dive into roadmaps and blueprints a little more before we go deeper into our *Joyful Copy* discussion.

19

DON'T COPY THAT

B y now, it should be clear that anyone who claims to be a Christ-follower and lives by the teachings of the Bible will never intentionally use an ounce of hype or manipulation in their marketing and copywriting. But don't just take my word for it. Let's back up this concept with a credible resource.

While many different reference guides and instruction books are available, one tool—already in your possession, by the way—has withstood the test of time. It is also the best-selling book of all time, which means the contents must be compelling and helpful. You and I call this book *the Bible*. But I also refer to *the Bible* as our Ultimate How-To Guide because it offers teaching and guidance for every aspect of our lives and businesses.

In turn, joyful copy follows God's Word to ensure the words used for marketing and copywriting mirror Christian characteristics instead of looking like the world. As you've been reading this book, you've probably noticed a few Scriptures that I've referenced many times. Specifically, I use Galatians 5:22–23 (the fruits of the Spirit passage) and Philippians 4:8 (the guide for our thought life) as litmus tests for determining whether copy aligns with God's Word. If any copy alludes to a characteristic, trait, or behavior opposite of those specific biblical elements, it is not joyful and needs to be revised.

While studying other marketers and copywriters will uncover some great insights about writing, you will easily see a consistent undercurrent of manipulation quietly creeping in to get people to take action. Sure, some people will dress up their words, make them look pretty, and create a distraction so you don't notice what is going on. They will also find ways to justify subtly using words as a hype-filled crowbar to open minds and wallets. Some of those same extremely talented people will also be quick to say one should never use copy or marketing to manipulate others. Ironically, they are using those very same tricks in plain sight while they distract their audience to look the other way. Unfortunately, today's carefully worded, high-pressure tactics used for (personal or client) gain are wrong.

Nowhere in God's Word does it say that a little bit of manipulation or hype is okay. Scripture spells out plainly that no form of manipulation should be part of any Christ-follower's world. These verses make that very clear:

- Don't take advantage of or do wrong to others (Leviticus 25:17).
- Gaining wealth by lying leads to death (Proverbs 21:6).
- Don't let anyone mislead you by using deceit (Matthew 24:4) .

For personal application, pause to think about the last time you were sucked into someone's marketing funnel. Whatever button you clicked probably caught your attention because the words you read or heard resonated with you. It probably felt like the writer was talking directly to you because they seemed to understand your needs and wants. (Pssst, there is nothing wrong with that technique. In fact, it is a powerful tool used by good copywriters and marketers.)

If you continued following the path to the seller's end goal and bought something, I'm hopeful you received what the seller offered. Sadly, the end result may have gone the other way. Perhaps you remember the sting of broken trust because of that time you bought into something that didn't deliver what it promised. (Yep, I've been there one too many times myself. So, I understand.)

One of the foundational concepts here is trust, which is vitally important in life and business because it offers safety, shows integrity, instills faith, and cements relationships. But once trust is lost, relationships weaken, and potential repeat buyers disappear. Sure, some entrepreneurs chalk up those occasional losses as the "cost of doing business" because they know there are other "fish" in the sea that will come to fill that gap. They may even become cavalier about those who figure out who they are and the vaporware they are actually selling. Sadly, those who operate this way have grown immune to the internal pleadings of their conscience to think, say, and do what is authentic and right. But it doesn't have to be that way.

When you partner with God in business, you'll possess a burning desire to always deliver on your promises to others. (Notice the adverb "always" in front of "deliver," which means all the time, not just when you remember or think about it.) When you partner with God in your business, you will make sure your "yes" means "yes" and your "no" means "no" (Matthew 5:37). Likewise, you will want to take steps to protect yourself by buying products, services, and solutions from authentic, aligned people who keep their word, too. (Sometimes that is easier said than done because people aren't always who they say they are.)

Just to make sure that the importance of who and what we trust is clear, God's Word mentions "trust" 134 times in the King James Version of the Bible. (For something to be mentioned that many times, it must be pretty important. Don't you think?!) While all of the verses on trust are notable, these two fit quite well here:

Trust is fragile like a spider's web. (Job 8:14a) Translation: Trust is broken in an instant. Sadly, trust has become a commodity that many trade for personal gain without a second thought.

Don't trade cleverness for riches. (Proverbs 23:4) Translation: Be careful not to follow the breadcrumb trail someone leaves because you think it will make you wealthy. For example, do not copy someone else's roadmap because they promise it will increase (XYZ-desirable aspect) of your business.

Remember, God made you unique with special gifts and talents that only you possess. In turn, the roadmap someone else has created for themselves will not work as well for you as it did for them. Sure, copying someone else's work might get you a little closer to your goal, but you're shortchanging yourself and the world of what God has prepared for you to do.

Now, please don't misunderstand what I'm saying. Learning from others who have experienced success or are experts in their field is not bad. It is good. Just like going to a doctor for help when you're sick, hiring a carpenter to build cabinets for your kitchen, or working with a coach to help you achieve XYZ, there are many resources that you should tap into to help you meet your goals.

What I'm suggesting is that no one should blatantly copy someone else's work, even if you paid them for the ability to use or copy it. Plagiarism—using someone else's words or ideas without giving them credit—is plagiarism no matter how you try to dress it up.

I'm reminded of a man who once took a writing certification class and submitted the words of another person. He copied someone else word-for-word and said it resulted from his own work. Upon review, it was obvious that the words were not his own, and the instructor confronted him. In mind-blowing defiance, the individual resolutely said he had a right to submit someone else's work as his own because he had paid for the ability to use that copy. Do what?! Yes, technically, the man had paid for someone else's sales page blueprint. But no one intended for him to submit that purchase as his work in a certification class, as it did not demonstrate his capability to write effective copy.

But copying someone else's work extends beyond plagiarism into roadmaps and blueprints. As we touched on before, it is a common practice to sell or buy detailed plans for doing pretty much anything today. A quick search through any inbox will find subject lines offering "blueprints for profitable product ideas," or "use my blueprint to scale to $500K in 1 year," or "$100K roadmap for making six figures," or "clear roadmap to tell you exactly what to do."

At face value, you may think nothing is wrong with any of those offers. Getting a step-by-step plan to follow like a recipe for success sounds like an easy pill to swallow. Guaranteed success and increased finances appear to create a win-win. Right?! But behind the scenes of those attention-getting words, something else is going on that is so subtly disguised it is easy to miss.

You see, following someone else's roadmap will keep your eye on *their* milestones and show you the path *they* took to reach *their* goals. In turn, you'll be distracted away from the specific path God has for you. When you pursue the transformation someone else made, you'll remain unchanged. You may even drift farther away from where God wanted you to go in the first place. The only guaranteed change you'll see from using someone else's roadmap will be in the loss of your funds and the time that you gave up. In turn, duplicating someone's blueprint creates a roadblock for Christ-followers because you unintentionally block the potential God wants to release in and through you. Copying someone else also makes it impossible for you to be authentic and genuine.

This concept takes me back to the early 80s when two friends and I decided to dress alike. (I don't remember why we did this, except we probably thought it would be cool.) It was easy to spot us during that school year because all three of us wore the same pink button-down Izod shirts, black skinny ties, pencil skirts, and penny loafers. It sounds silly thinking back on it, though the younger me probably thought we were the bomb. But in looking like each other, we lost our uniqueness, individuality, and voice. We were simply three copycats. Thankfully, our attire is where the copying stopped. As young teenagers, we were still stretching, growing, and learning to find our way in life. (And from what I've learned, the three of us eventually turned out alright.)

Here's what you need to focus on: As an entrepreneur, you already know that God has given you a vision for what He wants you to do. You may still be getting the download from Him. Or maybe you're slowly working out the details by executing a small piece at a time. But you know what He has called you to do and are learning how He wants you to show up in the marketplace. So, why would you interrupt that flow and get distracted by paying for some strangers' roadmaps that take you down a different path? Instead of copying the vision of others, turn to The Creator of all things. Ask Holy Spirit to lead you. Ask Him to give you strategies and frameworks to help you get where He wants you to go.

Everyone's Doing It, So It Must Be Okay

I can hear Daddy's voice like it was yesterday, "If Mary jumped off a bridge, would you jump too?" You see, Mary had taught me how to burp proudly and loudly. (In your childhood house burping might have been normal, but in my parents' house burping was similar to a death wish.) So you can imagine when I displayed my new burping skill at our very proper family dinner table, it went over like a lead balloon. But Daddy's question about following Mary wasn't far from the "everyone's doing it, so it must be okay" lie I had bought into as a young preteen.

Fast forward to today's "monkey see, monkey do" world, where the practice of copying others for success is an accepted norm. Unfortunately, blueprints for success divert Christ-followers' attention away from the Lord by enticing them with roadmaps that lead to wishful thinking and pie-in-the-sky realities.

These pipedream techniques are readily accepted and popular because we desire success and "everyone's doing it, so it must be okay." *Right?!* Wrong. In addition, those who offer these techniques are skilled at telling people what they want to hear with the singular intent of getting them to buy something at some point in time. Selling success in the form of roadmaps is a definite psychological ploy to get people to take action.

Consider this. When you duplicate someone else's blueprint, you may unknowingly copy an individual who:

- Drifted off course and isn't aligned with God anymore.
- Lives a double life with one foot in the world and one in the Bible.
- Views the teachings of the Bible as a Chinese menu with options from which you can pick and choose.
- Tainted the truth by mixing in a little subtle manipulation.
- Puts personal ambition and goals before a relationship with God.
- Practices bait-and-switch tactics with no remorse.

(By the way, each one of those bullet points describes the way I used to live at one point in time. I'm embarrassed to admit it, but it is important for you to know that I've lived on both sides. And like every single thing I've tried to do, I did each thing to the best of my ability.)

Here's the deal: Replicating someone else's work may find you unknowingly drinking tainted Kool-Aid. (Just a little poison doesn't hurt, does it?) As a result, you may travel in a different direction away from

God's best for you and your business without meaning to go off course.

Copying someone else jumps right over Abba Father's specific plans for your life. Why shortchange yourself of the blessings God has planned for you because you pursued a shortcut and copied someone else's roadmap?

Since you were uniquely made, His plans for you are also unique to you and no one else (Psalm 139:13–14 and 1 Peter 4:10). Instead of duplicating someone else, why not call out to Him and ask what He would have you do? Once you uncover Abba's plans for you, be intentional to share your message with your specific audience clearly, authentically, and ethically.

In today's "you do you" world, many view the teachings of the Bible as mere suggestions. Others see biblical principles as a cafeteria where you can pick and choose which items you want.

But those who strive to sincerely partner with Holy Spirit know that God's Word isn't filled with ala carte options. If you cherry-pick the principles that feel good to you or suit your needs, you open yourself up for failure. Similar to following a recipe for baking a cake, making things up as you go along doesn't work well. If you randomly leave out ingredients or guess instead of measuring, the end result will not taste very good.

If we are going to show up with Christian values, we want those values to permeate every aspect of our business and life. If you haven't done so already, let me encourage you to commit to ensuring that every word you speak and write is truthful, genuine, and aligned with God's Word.

Pause to think about your work for a moment. When prospects encounter your business, do they easily see God's light authentically shining through all you do? Or do they:

- Think you look similar to someone else?
- Experience lofty promises that you may or may not keep?
- Sense high-pressure sales tactics sprinkled with the fear of missing out?
- See through fake sincerity, phony interest, or ungenuine enthusiasm?
- Get sucked into wishful thinking and pipe dreams with unrealistic outcomes?

Let's look at specific ways to show up in the marketplace ethically and authentically.

20

YOU WILL KNOW
THEM BY THEIR FRUITS

Much has been written about people being known by their fruits and not their deeds. In fact, a quick online search pulls up many philosophers and thought leaders who have had much to say about that concept.

But the idea of being known by your fruits originated with Jesus. Let's look at some key points found in Matthew 7:15–20.

Jesus warned about false prophets who pretend to be sheep because they are wolves in disguise. Perhaps you've encountered people like this in business who say one thing to draw you in but are really saying "the right things" to get you to come into their web of deception and then act for their benefit. This behavior happens among believers and non-believers alike.

He pointed out that you will recognize these hypocrites by their contrived doctrine and self-focus (Matthew 7:16). When what someone shares sounds too good to be true or shines the light on **their** awesomeness, buyer beware because you're probably dealing with someone who isn't on the up and up.

The bow on top of this teaching shows up when Jesus compares identifying a tree by its fruits to identifying people by their actions. (Matthew 7:20) When you look closely at what others say and do, use discernment to make sure they are sincerely walking the talk and not just playing a game of smoke and mirrors to sell vaporware. Apply the same review process to everything you say and do. Keep in mind that some people don't realize their fruit is rotten because they've started believing their own lies.

Since writing copy with various forms of deception happens quite regularly, I felt compelled to research what others have to say about writing copy *without* hype. I intentionally used phrases like "ethical copy" and "ethical copywriting" in a quest to uncover insights into what others think.

While various perspectives surfaced, the following terms showed up consistently: authenticity, awareness, ethics, lies, manipulation, and oxymoron. According to some Google sources, the word pairings of "ethical copywriter" and "copywriting ethics" are considered contradictory terms. What I found made it apparent that many believe ethical copywriters are mythical creatures that do not exist.

Candidly, uncovering how many feel made my ethical copywriting toes curl. Why? Because not all writers use the same smarmy underhanded used car-salesmen tactics. Some copywriters, marketers, and business owners embrace their responsibility to ensure their words draw in the right customers in a trustworthy manner. Thank goodness all hope is not lost.

Here's the good news: If you strive to align your life and business with the teachings of *the Bible*, Holy Spirit will help your words convey truthfulness and hope without stretching or twisting reality. In turn, you'll be on the right path to consistently using ethical copywriting in your marketing.

But rest assured, just because you know what to do doesn't mean you will write all your copy ethically from here on out. Without realizing it, you can easily slip back into old habits of copying others and using subtle forms of hype and manipulation. If you don't stay focused on partnering with the Lord, you'll start to look like everyone else again. Remember, the evil one is on the prowl looking for opportunities to trip you up and pull you back into his way of doing things (1 Peter 5:8).

Using myself as an example, I feel compelled to tell you a personal story that demonstrates how easy it is to slip back into old ways. Nearly eight years ago, I decided to make a change. My fiftieth birthday was on the horizon when I realized I could be fit and fifty or fat and fifty. I opted for fit, which meant learning how to lift weights regularly and changing my diet to a Ketogains lifestyle. Over time, I transformed from a ladies' size eighteen to a size four/six. (So far, so good. Right?!)

That's when I became comfortable and took my eye off the prize. The pandemic hit, and while I worked out faithfully and still ate keto, I was sloppy about it. I threw caution to the wind and allowed myself to do lackluster workout routines that just went through the motions. So what if I had an entire bag of pork rinds while I wrote for clients. My justification was it helped me think better. The results of my dirty keto started to show, and a visit with my doctor helped me realize I was headed back in the wrong direction.

I'm happy to say that, as of this writing, I'm back in the saddle and following the protocols that I know work for me. (Translation: Strict keto, macro tracking, and Ketogains weightlifting generates the results I need, want, and desire.) Today, you can look at me and physically see the fruits of my labor and hard work.

Similar to consistently following a diet, tracking what you eat, and working out six days a week, you need to intentionally keep your focus on your partnership with God while consistently reviewing what you write for biblical alignment and eliminating any subtle forms of twisted reality. Let's look at how the fruits of your life and your marketing labor can showcase biblical truths.

Mirror the Right Person

At some point in time, most people seek and desire peer acceptance. Some make it a lifelong quest, while others are sucked into that vortex only temporarily as teenagers. It makes me think about growing up in the 70s and begging my mom to buy me earth shoes, puka shells, and many cans of Aqua Net hairspray to go with my feathered haircut. Why? Because I wanted people to like me, so modifying the way I talked, looked, and behaved to mirror "the cool kids" was important to me.

You may find that "mirroring the cool entrepreneurs" is what you're doing in your business and life even today. "Keeping up with the Joneses" is a real phenomenon. I've worked with many who have struggled because they allowed the success of others to distract them, cloud their focus, and pull them in a different direction. (I know how easily that happens because I've been there, too.)

Alternatively, what if you followed our Creator's Ultimate How-To Guide instead of mirroring the many success stories available in the world? You would definitely look different and stand out from everyone else. In turn, the right people would be drawn to you and want to know what makes you different. Talk about a golden opportunity to share His love and light.

Let me encourage you to stay focused on what God wants you to do and follow His lead. Don't be concerned about what other entrepreneurs or small business owners write, do, or say. When you focus on the right things, you'll achieve more than you ever imagined possible. (Trust me. Better yet, trust God.)

Ensure Your Copy Is Joyful

One of the best ways to produce joyful copy is by making sure whatever you think, say, and do is ethical and aligned with God's Word. It is easier than you think. And the more you practice this principle, the stronger you'll become in taking a stand the right way.

While the Bible is overflowing with sage counsel and training, three core Scriptures point out the best ways for Christ-followers to think, speak and act in every aspect of life and business. We've touched these verses many times along the way, but let's walk through each passage again.

- Ephesians 5:1–10 gives specific instructions about living in the Light by showing others love, goodness, righteousness, truth, wisdom, and gratitude.

- Galatians 5:22–23 outlines Christian characteristics (aka the fruits of the Spirit): love, joy, peace, patience, kindness, gentleness, faithfulness, goodness, and self-control.

- Philippians 4:8 addresses what we should think about and focus on—specifically, what is true, honorable, right, pure, lovely, and admirable.

Notice how those emotions and characteristics are not negative, disparaging, or pessimistic. Each trait edifies, encourages, and lifts up. None of those Christlike attributes create the agitation, distress, or deception that subtly hides within much business copy today.

When I realized the differences, I spent countless hours comparing how I wrote for clients to the specific directions God's Word gives us. Trying to make this distinction on my own seemed overwhelming and hard. But conversations with Abba Father helped me see an easy way for anyone who follows Him to show up in the world authentically by applying some Holy Spirit-given wisdom and discernment.

Here's the secret: If you want your copy to be joyful, then filter what you've written through Scripture. *Joyful Copy* seeks to imitate the biblical characteristics found in the passages I referenced earlier.

Once you understand the premise, creating joyful copy is quite simple. After you've written the copy for a project, pause to check for biblical alignment and make edits where needed. The best way to uncover words and phrases that don't line up is by filtering your words through Galatians 5:22–23 and Philippians 4:8. If you find something that does not show those godly characteristics, you'll want to revise or rewrite the passage completely. If you find a segment that possesses even a hint of hype or a dash of manipulation, then it is time to edit and make what you write right. (Just a little play on words - make what you write right. Ha! Get it?!)

Let's walk through the steps for making what you write joyful in today's marketplace.

- **Review.** After you've written your copy, thoughtfully filter it through Christian characteristics found in Scripture.

- **Revise.** Rewrite any sentence, phrase, or section that uses subtle hype or doesn't align with God's Word.

- **Remove.** Extract anything that uses twisted realities or creates a false sense of need to encourage people to act.

- **Reject.** Sometimes you may need to throw out what you've written and start over.

To make it easy for you to check for joyful alignment, I created a simple checklist that you can use. In the left column are Joyful Characteristics that you should find in whatever content you create. On the right are hype-filled nuances to eliminate. You can refer to the *Joyful Copy Checklist* here in the book and also download a free copy here: https://www.joycapps.com/joyful-copy-alignment

Since I frequently update this checklist with tweaks here and there as Holy Spirit leads, you may want to periodically check that link or reach out to me to ensure you have the latest version.

Joyful Copy Checklist

Hey there,

When you see the success others experience in today's marketplace, you may find it tempting to mirror the way they write and market their business.

Following someone's roadmap is easy, BUT you may start using manipulation, hype, and control tactics without even realizing it.

Sure, those psychological tricks will get people to take action, spend money, and do various things. But at what cost?!

Manipulation is easy to do, but there's a better way to do things.

While you may learn great marketing and writing concepts from other entrepreneurs and teachers, it is important to run everything you use through The Ultimate How-To Manual (aka The Bible) to check for alignment.

If you see any marketing technique or writing framework that doesn't align with Biblical principles, consider it a danger sign.

Embrace the opportunity to take a stand, be different, and shine God's light in a dark world. Make sure every word that is written or said about your business is joyful.

One way to do this is by running your words through this Joyful Copy Checklist. Let's look at how you will use this simple tool.

Joy

www.JoyCapps.com

Is Your Copy Joyful or Hype-Filled?

The list of attributes on the next page are based on two passages found in Galatians and Philippians.

Galatians 5:22-23: But the fruit of the Spirit is love, joy, peace, forbearance, kindness, goodness, faithfulness, gentleness and self-control. *(See blue highlighted words on next page)*

Philippians. 4:8: Whatever is true, whatever is noble, whatever is right, whatever is pure, whatever is lovely, whatever is admirable—if anything is excellent or praiseworthy—think about such things. *(See grey highlighted words on next page)*

If your copy is aligned with these attributes, then there should be no hype. In turn, your copy should be joyful.

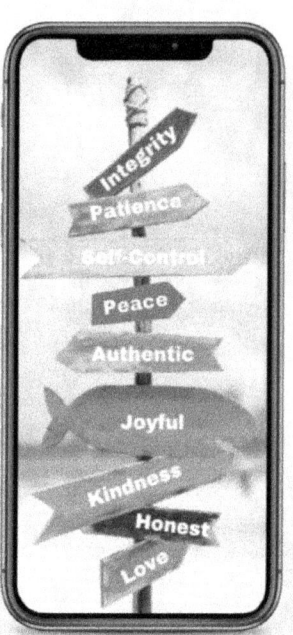

● ●

<u>How to Use the Joyful Copy Checklist</u>

ONE: Review what you've written to see if your copy is joyful or hints at twisted realities or subtle manipulations.

TWO: If you find words, phrases, or paragraphs that aren't joyful, then rewrite that section to remove any hype and ensure joyfulness.

www.JoyCapps.com

Joyful Copy Checklist

Joyful	Hype
Authentic, Pure	Dishonest, Embellished, Fake
Considerate, Gentle	Abrasive, Combative, Defiant
Genuine, Faithful	Hypocrisy, Insincere, Phony
Honest, Right	Corrupt, Fraudulent, Inaccurate
Honorable, Noble	Devious, Dishonest, Unethical
Integrity, Good	Deceitful, Manipulative, Trickery
Joy	Depressed, Negative
Kindness	Harsh, Hostile, Thoughtless
Love	Anger, Fear, Selfishness
Patient, Easy-Going	Cynical, Impatient, Vengeful
Peaceful	Anxious, Apathetic, Worrisome
Pleasant, Lovely	Agitated, Gloomy, Offensive
Praiseworthy, Admirable	Loathsome, Repulsive, Shameful
Self-Controlled	Impulsive, Manipulative, Hype

www.JoyCapps.com

To understand this concept better, think about the tires on your car. You drive along the road without issues until something happens that throws your tires out of alignment, then your car doesn't ride as smoothly. You may not feel it at first, but it becomes evident that something isn't quite right after a while. When that happens, you ask a mechanic to check out the situation. After troubleshooting, they usually recommend an alignment. But, sometimes, they will tell you that your tires are a lost cause and you need to replace them. Out with the old, in with the new. Just like evaluating tires, you need to review your marketing to make sure what you're creating and putting out in the world flows smoothly with God's Word.

If you've decided to partner with Holy Spirit in your business, you need to review everything you've created to see if anything might not align. Sometimes a simple tweak will put us back into alignment, but other times, we have to throw out the entire project and start over.

Wherever you find yourself in your journey, let me encourage you to take the time to review what you've created. Make sure your copy, content, courses, books, products, and services are joyful. If you find any hype, take the necessary steps to revise and make it right.

By partnering with Abba Father consistently, you're giving God the freedom to bless you for honoring Him. But don't take my word for it. In Luke 11:28, Jesus said: "Blessed are those who hear the word of God and obey it." It couldn't be any plainer than that. God is calling us to consistently show up in life and the marketplace authentically.

PART IV
REFLECTION QUESTIONS

Some of these questions may be hard to answer or make you uncomfortable. But just like learning a new skill, changing your diet, or (insert challenging thing here), change is hard. As they say, "no pain, no gain."

Let me encourage you to pause, reflect, and honestly answer each question before moving forward.

Points to Ponder

When you market your business or sell to others, do you copy blueprints from others? Do you feel successful? Or does it make you feel like you're faking it until you make it?

What compels you to copy others instead of finding ways to shine God's light through your words?

Do you see God's Word as a pick-and-choose menu of suggestions? Why or why not?

When prospects encounter your work or business, do they easily see God's light authentically shining through all you do? Or do they:

- Sense high-pressure sales?
- Experience lofty promises?
- See pie-in-the-sky realities?
- Get sucked into wishful thinking?

What can you do to make sure you align the marketing you create with God's Word?

PART V: HOW TO IDENTIFY COPY THAT CONNECTS

The following chapters will walk you through the process I use to uncover what's important to an audience and their language so I know what to write.

As you read through Parts V-VII, please keep the following in mind:

- This content is not a blueprint to success. It is shared as a framework to guide you.

- True success will happen only when you partner with Holy Spirit in all you think, say, and do.

- Connecting with your customers involves listening to what your prospects and customers have to say, showing you understand, and offering solutions that address their needs.

- Connecting with others authentically, ethically, and joyfully involves partnering with Holy Spirit and filtering what you write through the Ultimate How-To Guide (aka the Bible).

- Nothing shared here is original content because I've learned it through trial and error, studying others, seeking direction from Holy Spirit, and using the Ultimate How-To Guide.

- If you cherry-pick portions of the following frameworks to use, you may not experience the results or success you desire for connecting with your customers.

Writing copy that connects with your customers involves:

- Determining what's important to your audience.
- Distilling your message by using engaging language.
- Delivering results by pulling it all together and making sure it is joyfully aligned.

To set you up for success, let's start by looking at how to design your game plan.

21

DESIGN YOUR GAMEPLAN

The best way to start anything is by posturing and partnering with God, then following His lead to design what you'll create. Here's what I strive to do in my business and life:

Before I work on any project, I talk to God about it. I ask Him to renew me by filling me with His Holy Spirit and help me hear His voice in ALL I think, say, and do. Next—and here's the key—I ask Him to help me take action on it. Then I set out to obey what Holy Spirit impresses me to do.

Remember that this isn't a ritual, checklist, or a one-and-done. This quest is a continual, ongoing process that finds me seeking God for advice and input throughout each day. Why? Because it is easy to become distracted or start to work on my own. When that happens, I easily get derailed and go off course. (Think shiny object syndrome or… squirrel!)

While this process has become a daily part of my routine, my humanity gets in the way ALL. THE. TIME.

What do I mean by humanity? The terms "pride" and "rebellion" come to mind. You know, when I act like, "I've got this. I'll let You know when I need help, Abba." Or sometimes I display the "I have arrived" mentality. "Watch what I can do." Maybe I've allowed the world to distract me or, worse yet, I've tried to please a client before pleasing God. *(Yep, I'm guilty of all those things and more.)*

If I took inventory of the countless times I've tried to compartmentalize God, I would be embarrassed. Or the numerous times I've created something on my own, without His input, and then expected Him to bless it. *(What a disaster!)*

Thankfully, He is always patiently waiting for me to come back and involve Him in my planning.

Here are a few paraphrases of core verses that come to mind about involving God in all you do. If you were a fly on the wall of my mind, you'd see that I've memorized each verse and recite them many times throughout my workday. You may want to do the same.

- Commit your plans to the Lord, so He will direct your steps and help you succeed (Proverbs 16:3, 9).

- Put ALL your trust in Him without leaning into your understanding, and He will show you which way to go (Proverbs 3:5–6).

- Call out to Him, and He WILL show you what He's been waiting to reveal to you (Jeremiah 33:3).

[ACTION STEP] If you ask Abba Father specific questions about what you write, create, and do in your work, He WILL help you. If you ask for His guidance, He WILL show up in ways greater than you ever imagined. (Don't take my word for it. Try it.) Please consider pausing for a moment to add your responses to your journal.

Once you make sure that Abba Father has a seat at the head of your table, work through specific frameworks to write joyful copy that will connect, educate, persuade, and sell.

Are You Doing Your Part?

Before you move forward, let's address a question that I've heard a lot over the years. Many Christ-following entrepreneurs ask me: Won't Holy Spirit tell me what to write? If so, why do I need to learn how to write joyfully?

Yes, I agree that Holy Spirit will put words, tactics, and strategies in your heart and mind. But I also know that He expects us to do our part.

When we get sick, we pray and ask God to heal us. But we don't just sit still and wait for a miracle to happen. We also visit a doctor that God equipped with wisdom and knowledge to help us get better.

The same happens with every facet of your business—copywriting, marketing, coaching, sales strategy, videography, social media, or (insert business tactic here).

Following God's lead, you need to seek to understand the gap or problems your customers possess that your solutions solve. You need to get a handle on the opportunities your prospects desire and show how your services will help them achieve those goals. When you do, He will help you design a plan.

If you think about it, Jesus used the same approach. Granted, His Omnipotence means He knows our problems without conducting research like we need to do. But while Jesus walked this earth, His encounters with others found Him focused on someone's problem, showing He understood and offering an opportunity to embrace His solution. Sure, His solution is life-changing for eternity. You and I cannot begin to compare what we offer in business to Salvation. But, you can use a similar approach that focuses on your customers' problems, showcases your understanding, and provide opportunities for transformational solutions to solve those issues.

You won't address about ALL their problems or gaps. You'll talk about the very specific issues that you solve and opportunities you create through your business offerings.

In the case of your business products and services, you know there are problems your customer needs to solve. You also know they are seeking opportunities that you can help them find and fulfill.

The key is researching and listening to understand your customers' problems, language, objections, needs, wants, and desires. Ask Holy Spirit to give you ears to hear what He hears.

Before we move forward, I need to reiterate and emphasize something so it is clear: This process is not original or unique. It is not a cookie-cutter roadmap to follow either. The *Joyful Copy* process emerged from my partnership with Abba Father and years of studying copywriting techniques from master copywriters in the field. My partnership with God and learning from others is never-ending.

Do I copy what I see others do? Absolutely NOT.

Just like learning to do anything, I study the final products someone created, assess the ingredients, watch their techniques, and then find ways to turn what I've learned into something unique to me. You should do likewise.

Building Your Reservoir of Information

The first step for any aspect of a Christ-following entrepreneur's marketing and copywriting involves spending time partnering with the Lord. I've already written about how I do this at the beginning of this section.

Every copywriter and business owner follows a process for writing. I base my process on collecting information and applying specific copywriting techniques with Holy Spirit's guidance. (Yes, I am repeating myself. But I believe it is easier to remember what we hear repeatedly.)

The next sections and exercises are designed to help you by uncovering key information about your customers, business, solutions, and competitors. You may think you already know the answers to these questions, but when you take the time to really dig in, you may be surprised by what you uncover.

While each exercise requires an investment of time to complete, I promise you the pay-off is worth it because it will make writing copy a breeze in the future.

Your Reservoir of Information Exercise

[ACTION STEP] Start building your Reservoir of Information.

HERE'S WHAT TO DO: Create a folder on your computer or cloud-based drive where you write and store your findings. Clearly label the information so it is easy to understand what each document contains. Doing so will help you quickly pull insights from your Reservoir of Information into future copy that you need to write.

22

DETERMINE: FIND THE KEYS TO UNLOCK DOORS

Have you ever wished there was an easy way to figure out what to write about your business? You're not alone because countless entrepreneurs have expressed the same thought to me over the years.

You can easily determine what will interest potential customers. In fact, I've worked with many who've achieved great success over the years because they've rolled up their sleeves and done what it takes to determine which keys unlock the prospects' and customers' doors.

Sadly, I've noticed that many entrepreneurs think they know and understand their audience when they don't. I've even worked with a small number of people who have fought this part of the process, refused to do it, and thus failed to achieve the results they needed.

Word to the Wise: Do NOT skip or sail through this stage if you want to know what to write. WHY? Because every step shared here is intentional to help you gain understanding as you work through what Abba Father had you design in partnership with Him.

Remember the baking analogy? When you're following a recipe, you don't skip a step or leave out an ingredient because it will mess up the finished product. While I'm definitely not a baker, I know that leaving baking soda out of a cookie or cake recipe is asking for trouble and won't achieve the desired results. That same concept applies here, too.

The Determine Process helps you look at your business and potential customers from several angles. It involves reviewing what you think you understand and listening to your prospects and customers.

Before you move forward, I need to let you know that this first step about your perceptions may stretch you. Some of my *Joyful Copy Camp* students and Done-WITH-You clients have shed tears as they walked through this exercise.

While tears are not my goal, I want to encourage you to take time to reflect and pray about each step as you work through writing joyful copy.

At this point, let's take a quick detour and touch on your mindset. WHY? Because you may encounter mindset issues at one point or another and not realize what's really going on.

Whose Voice Are You Hearing?

It is important to use heavenly wisdom and discernment as your filter and guide when you navigate through life, work on your business, and strive to write joyful copy.

Any stressors that you feel as you walk through life and business, as well as these copywriting and marketing exercises, are not from the Lord. How do I know that? Because there is a clear difference between Satan's voice and God's voice.

In short, here's what you and I both know to be true: God's voice will lift you and help you soar on wings like eagles (Isaiah 40:31), while

Satan's voice is like a roaring lion seeking whom he may devour (1 Peter 5:8).

God's Voice	Satan's Voice
Calms You	Obsesses You
Comforts You	Worries You
Convicts You	Condemns You
Encourages You	Discourages You
Enlightens You	Confuses You
Leads You	Pushes You
Reassures You	Frightens You
Stills You	Rushes You

As you work through these exercises, stop each step of the way and ask God to partner with you and guide you. When you lean into Him and not your own understanding, He WILL direct your paths (Proverbs 3:5–6). (You can take that promise to the bank.)

If you feel any negative emotions, pause to pray about it. Turn the situation over to God. Ask Him to fill you with joy unspeakable, and He will. (See 1 Peter 1:8.)

23

WHAT DO YOU SEE?

I t all begins with YOUR perception of your customers, business, and competitors.

Your Perceptions Exercise

[ACTION STEP] (Add your responses to this exercise to your Reservoir of Information.)

HERE'S WHAT TO DO: Carve out some time to reflect on each of those three groups, and write what you think the response is to the following questions.

Your Perception about Your Customers

- What problem/pain points do your ideal customers have that your solutions solve? (List them all.)

- What opportunities and goals do your ideal customers desire that your solutions will help them reach?

- What values are they committed to in their life and business? Do they elevate those values or keep them hidden from view?

- What is their mindset and attitude towards the problems THEY experience that you solve?

- Do they have predisposed beliefs or opinions? Aspirations? Dreams?

- How does your business align or support any of their beliefs, aspirations, or dreams?

- When they search for solutions like yours, what objections might they share or keep to themselves?

- Are there particular questions they tend to ask when you're talking to them about their problems and goals or your solutions?

- Do they have a personal relationship with Jesus, or is that topic dicey with them?

- How do you think Abba Father views their pain points or the opportunities they desire? Is there anything He wants them to know about these issues and desires?

Your Perception about Your Business

- What problem/pain points do your solutions solve for your customers? (List them all.)

- What opportunities and goals do your ideal customers want your business solutions to help them achieve?

  - Is that realistic or outside the scope of what you've envisioned with the Lord?

  - Do you need to make tweaks to your solutions based on these insights?

- What values are YOU committed to in your life and business? Do you elevate those values or keep them hidden from view?

- What is your mindset and attitude towards your customers' issues that you solve? Do you perceive their challenges as trivial burdens, growth opportunities, or (insert your perception of their issue here)?

- What are YOUR predisposed beliefs or opinions? Aspirations? Dreams? Do you showcase those in your business?

- When you engage in sales convos with prospects, what objections do you hear frequently?

- Are there particular questions prospects tend to ask? (List them all.)

- Do you have a personal relationship with Jesus? Or do you view Him as an option that you pull out whenever you need something?

- Do you elevate your convictions and beliefs through your business? If so, how?

- How do you think Abba Father views what you offer through your business? Is there anything He wants you to know about your business and the solutions you provide others? (If you're not sure, pause to ask Him, and listen to what He shares.)

Your Perception about Your Competitors

- What problem/pain points do your competitors' solutions solve? (List them all.)

- Do your ideal customers want the same results from your competitors' business solutions that they want from yours?

- What opportunities and goals do their business solutions help potential customers achieve?

- How is what they offer different from your solutions?

- In what ways is what they offer better?

- Are there gaps in what they offer that your solutions fill?

- What values are your competitors committed to in their lives and businesses? How do those values differ from yours?

- What are your competitors' mindsets and attitudes towards the problems your customers experience that both your businesses solve?

- Are your competitors authorities on the problems because they have experienced them, too?

- Or do they view the problems and opportunities as simple ways to make money?

- Do your competitors have predisposed beliefs or opinions? Aspirations? Dreams?

- Do they allow their beliefs, aspirations, and dreams to show up in their businesses?

- When they engage in sales convos with prospects, what objections do you think they hear frequently?

- Are there particular questions you think prospects tend to ask them?

- Do your competitors have a personal relationship with Jesus, or is that topic dicey with them?

- Do your competitors elevate their convictions and beliefs through their businesses? If so, how?

- How do you think Abba Father views what they do? Is there anything He wants you to know about their business and the solutions they provide? (If you're not sure, ask Him.)

Once you've written out your perceptions, you'll want to set that document aside. You'll revisit it again shortly.

24

VALIDATING
YOUR PERCEPTIONS

Now that you've written out your perceptions, it is time to confirm what you think you know. Research is the best way to validate your viewpoints about your customers and competitors.

In addition to conducting online research where you observe and learn your customers' language, I recommend conducting two different kinds of surveys with your audience and doing SWOT analyses on your competitors.

Let's walk through how to do all three.

SWOT Your Competition

When I say competitors, more than ninety percent of the time, business owners respond with, "But I'm unique and don't have any competitors."

I agree that God made each one of us uniquely. But I counter that unless you're an inventor, someone out there is offering something similar to your product or service. Sure, it may not mirror what you offer, but it is probably close enough that their business would qualify as a competitor.

At the end of the day, we see three basic types of competitors: direct, indirect, and replacement. Let's take a look at each type:

- Direct competitors offer the same products, services, and solutions you offer, AND they have the same end game.

- Indirect competitors offer the same things, but their goals differ from yours.

- Replacement competitors offer something someone could use instead of choosing your product.

SWOT Exercise Step 1

[ACTION STEP] (Add your responses to this exercise to your Reservoir of Information.)

To SWOT Your Competition, you need to evaluate the **S**trengths, **W**eaknesses, **O**pportunities, and **T**hreats of your business and those you consider your competition. You may even want to do a SWOT analysis for a business you admire that you'd like to learn from as your business grows.

HERE'S WHAT TO DO: Pause to think about what you're offering in today's marketplace. Then think about your competitors as they fall into one or all of those competitor descriptions. Ask Holy Spirit to help you select three to five companies you consistently compete with or run up against in business. Better yet, ask Holy Spirit to help you pick some you would like to emulate or compete with one day.

To make this work well, be sure you're looking at companies similar in size and offerings to your business. For example:

- If you're in real estate, look at realtors near you that serve a similar market with an equal number of agents and brokers.

- If you're a bakery or medical clinic, do the same thing.

- If you're only serving your audience online, your reach is wider, so you can look at others who have similar offerings anywhere online.

- Lastly, you may want to look at a business that, though it isn't nearby, you admire and would like to emulate some of the ways they do things.

SWOT Exercise Step 2

[ACTION STEP] (Add your responses to this exercise to your Reservoir of Information.)

HERE'S WHAT TO DO: Block out time to do this SWOT exercise thoroughly by researching the three to five competitors you chose. You may look online, go to their store, subscribe to their email list, and look on social media. Seek out places where more information about them is available.

Fill out this form for each of your selected competitors.

- Name of Company:
- Website:
- Tagline:
- Products and Services:

Strengths *What THEY are good at doing	Weaknesses *An area THEY are lacking in or don't represent well
• •	• •

Opportunities *A gap THEY (or you) could fill in their marketplace	Threats *Something THEY are doing that you know you should be doing
• •	• •

Objections/Hesitations *Objections you think they hear from prospects
• •

SWOT Exercise Step 3

[ACTION STEP] (Add your responses to this exercise to your Reservoir of Information.)

HERE'S WHAT TO DO: Once you complete this exercise, go back and look for areas where your business can take a stand and shine brightly. You may recognize things your business already does that you haven't elevated. You may also see opportunities for what you know you could do but haven't created yet.

Use the knowledge you uncover to position your business strongly and strategically. Ask Holy Spirit to help you use this information to see things you haven't recognized in the past. If you analyze the results well, you'll find areas that will help you measure your success. You may also identify potential growth strategies you need to implement.

Ask Your Customers

As a preacher's kid, I've spent a lifetime watching my evangelist dad and pastor grandfather try to get people to come to church. While I could unpack all the methods they employed over the years to grow their attendance numbers, one key lesson is tangential to what you need to do to grow your business: take the time to ask.

Time and time again, when my dad asked a new guest what made them come to visit the church, the answer was the same: "Because someone asked me to come."

Now that may sound too simple, but the fact of the matter is most people don't visit a church because no one asked them. (Hard to believe. Right?!)

What does asking people to come to church have to do with you and writing joyful copy for your business? Two things:

Plant Seeds

If you haven't already, ask people you know—neighbors, colleagues, and friends—to come to church with you or learn more about your business solutions. You may get many "No, thank you" responses, but the occasional "Yes, I'd love to" responses are worth it all. Besides, you're planting seeds about what you offer every time you ask.

Uncover and Validate Insights

When you want to write good copy and validate what you think you know about your customers, you need to ask them what is important to them. Once you ask a handful of people the same questions, compare results to look for patterns.

Never make assumptions or think you know everything about your customers. Even if you've been doing the same line of work or offering similar solutions for a decade, it is important to reach out and validate what you think you know. WHY? Because people are constantly changing their viewpoints, needs, wants, and desires.

I recommend two ways to find commonalities in your customers: interviews and surveys.

Sometimes people interview five to ten people first and use those answers to shape their surveys. (This approach is the one I recommend doing, if possible.)

Other times, people don't have the luxury of time, so they do both the interviews and surveys in tandem. (This approach will work, but it does require that you project a bit of what you think you know into the survey questions.)

Let's walk through this process step by step.

Interview Your Customers Live

Interviewing customers and prospects will reveal to you valuable insights you may not know, as well as validate what you thought you knew. The interviews can happen over the phone, via Zoom, or in person. The answers to these questions will validate your perceptions and create a running list of content you can write about or create products for when the time comes.

Customer Interviews Step 1

[ACTION STEP] (Add your responses to this exercise to your Reservoir of Information.)

HERE'S WHAT TO DO: I recommend you select five to ten people you think would be willing to talk to you and send them an email telling them what you're trying to do.

Here's what you'll need to do:

- Compile a list of five to ten people who will share insights with you.
- Consider reaching out to former customers or prospective customers.
- Use Uber Conference or Zoom so that you can record the conversations. Both have free options available.
- Prepare well-thought-out questions before the calls.
- Make sure the phone interview questions are open-ended.
- Use the same questions on each call.

If you're not sure who to ask, or even if you already have your list in mind--let me encourage you to pray about it. Ask Abba Father to bring to mind who He wants you to reach out to for an interview. Or you may ask Him to help you see who He wants you to remove from or add to your list.

The email and questions you will want to use will look something like these examples. NOTE: While I'm sharing examples with you here, I ask that you use this only as a guide; customize the words to fit your audience and needs. Translation: Don't copy and paste what I've written here.

Target Audience:	Interview/Phone Convo Request
From:	Your Name
From Email:	Your Email Address
Subject Line Options:	<ul><li>Would you do me a favor?</li><li>I need your help, {{first name}}</li><li>Could you spare 15 minutes?</li></ul>
Links:	To your calendar, if you have one to share

Hi, (First Name),

(Personalize the greeting so it sounds like you. You might say something like: *It's been a while since we last connected*, or *Long time no chat*.)

I was thinking about you because I'm (describe what you're doing, e.g., researching what is important to my customers), and you're the type of person who (has benefited in the past/could benefit from what I'm offering OR I'd enjoy collaborating with/supporting you).

While I have ideas, your insights could help me validate them during my research phase.

Would you mind hopping on a call with me for about 15 minutes?

Here is a link to my calendar, where you can sign up for a call at the time that works best for you! (OR Let me know if this works for you, and we'll find a mutual time that is convenient to chat.)

Talk soon.

(Use your typical email signature close),

(Insert Your Name)

Live Interview Questions

Gentle Reminder: Try to record the conversation to listen to it later. (If you're a visual learner like me, make it easy on yourself by sending the recording to an AI-based transcription service like Temi.)

Customer Interviews Step 2

[ACTION STEP] (Add your responses to this exercise to your Reservoir of Information.)

HERE'S WHAT TO DO: Customize each of the following questions to your business BEFORE you interview someone. Pray over the questions and ask God to help you make sure you didn't miss anything.

Note that some of these questions ask the same thing in different ways. Sometimes that is needed to help you get an answer you can use. When you feel you have already collected what you need, you may choose to skip a question.

- What are your biggest challenges and frustrations when it comes to (the areas your products and solutions solve)?

- What keeps you up at night about (insert specific problems they have or an opportunity they want you to solve)?

- What do you value most about (insert the specific problem you solve)?

- What are the three biggest issues around (specific problem you solve) that you're currently struggling with or have struggled with in the past?

- How does having these problems make you feel?

- What specific things have you tried to overcome these problems?

- Why do you think these things haven't worked?

- What would it look like if you could wave your magic wand to create a perfect (problem you solve)?

- How will you feel if (XYZ problems) don't get better in the next year?

- How would you feel if you were in the same place one year from now?

- How would your life be different if you could solve (this problem)?

- How would you feel if (XYZ problem) were no longer an issue you needed to resolve?

- BONUS QUESTION if the person has worked with you in the past: If you were going to recommend working with (you or your business name), what would you say?

- May I share your recommendation online?

Before you interview someone, pause to ask Abba Father to join you in the conversation. Ask Him to guide how the interview flows and help you uncover insights you didn't know existed.

- Once you get on the call, thank the person for their time.

- Tell them you're recording the call for internal purposes only and to help you remember what they share.

- To move the call along, say something like, "I want to respect your time, so if you're okay with it, let's jump into the questions."

- If the person you're interviewing is quiet, don't try to fill the dead space. Allow some silence to pass. They may be thinking about your question, and if you speak up instead of giving them time to reflect, you may unintentionally influence their response.

Customer Interviews Step 3

[ACTION STEP] (Add your responses to this exercise to your Reservoir of Information.)

HERE'S WHAT TO DO: Once you complete all your interviews, you'll want to compare what you heard to:

- Find common themes and insights shared consistently through the many interviews.

- Pull out common language and terminology your customers use.

- Influence and shape the online survey you'll create and distribute.

If you were able to do live interviews before creating an online survey, use the commonalities to shape the choices that you will give for each online survey question.

Survey Your Customers

Many resources and tools are available for conducting surveys. You can spend a LOT of money paying someone to create and conduct the surveys for you. If you're really into it, many courses and books are available to teach you how to make surveying the focal point of what you offer.

While those resources have merit and have created great success for many, what I'm recommending is easier on your wallet and simple to conduct on your own.

Here's what you'll need:

- An email list of customers and prospects (any size will work, but the larger, the better)

- A survey tool
- An email service provider to send out your emails
- A short email sequence to get people to take your survey
- A giveaway to entice and reward people who participate
- The survey you create
- A short window for taking the survey

Let's break down each item:

Email List

Any size list will work, but the larger, the better. I recommend you try to email at least 100 people, especially since only a percentage of people will participate in the survey. Many variables weigh into how many people will respond. With very cold email lists that you haven't reached out to in a long time, I've seen fewer than 10 percent respond. But I've also seen as many as 70 percent respond, too.

When creating your email list, make sure you have permission to email each person. Otherwise, your people will perceive your email as spam. Additionally, according to the CAN-SPAM Act, it is illegal. If you're not familiar with this law, please take a moment to look it up because you are accountable whether you are familiar with the law or not.

Just make sure the people you're emailing are part of your target audience for the products and services you sell. Former and prospective customers are good choices.

Make sure you pray about the list you pull together. Ask the Lord if there are people you need to add or perhaps remove. The key is pausing to listen for His voice instead of rushing through the process.

Survey Tool

With a goal of including only ten questions or less, I recommend you use the free versions of Google Forms, Typeform, or Survey Monkey. Either tool will serve your needs well. (If you find using the technology challenging you, reach out to me, and I'll do what I can to guide you through the process. Seriously, send me a note at Joy@JoyCapps.com or find me on Facebook.)

Email Service Provider (ESP)

A large percentage of small business owners use the free version of Mail Chimp. In contrast, others use platforms like ActiveCampaign, AWeber, ConvertKit, Deadline Funnels, Drip, iContact, Kajabi, etc. The key is picking one platform and sticking with it, so your emails are recognized and not diverted to spam. If you suffer from shining-object syndrome and jump from one ESP to another, you may find your emails never make it into inboxes because they get blocked.

Email Sequence

You'll want to push out emails inviting people to participate in the survey, reminding them to take the survey, and thanking them for participating. I've included examples below the survey. Since your survey doesn't connect to most ESPs behind the scenes, you'll need to recognize that some people may have already participated in the survey in your emails. (This sentence will make more sense when you read through the email examples shared below the survey.)

Free Giveaway

I recommend that you include a gift for participating in the survey because most people need a reason to complete it. Some people offer a free one-to two-page download of something your audience would consider useful and valuable. Others have given access to a training video or podcast recording. I've even seen people offer discounts or a free ebook. The choice is yours. Think about your audience and what they will consider valuable.

Some people also include a drawing for something of monetary value. For example, you may enter survey participants in a drawing for one of two $50 Amazon gift cards. My clients have offered a Visa gift card for dinner and a movie or the latest cool gadget. One deep-pocketed client actually dangled the carrot of an iPad. I recommend you offer what makes sense to your audience and your budget.

Timing

Finally, let's chat about the time window for taking the survey. I recommend that you open the survey one morning and close participation three days later by the end of the day.

Translation: You want a very short window for participation so people participate while it is fresh on their minds. People will have good intentions and forget about it if you give a long window.

For example, if your audience is most active online mid-week, consider opening the survey Tuesday morning and closing it by the end of the day Thursday. If your audience is most active over the weekend, you'll want to open the survey on a Thursday or Friday and close it the following Sunday. If you don't know which days your audience is most active, just put a stake in the ground and stick with it.

The Survey

Now that you've planned everything out, you'll want to create the survey. You'll use common responses to shape your questions if you've done the interviews first. If you're doing both live interviews and the online survey in tandem, you need to realize that you are, in essence, influencing responses by shaping their choices with your thoughts. Again, I recommend using Google Forms, Typeform, or Survey Monkey.

Customer Interviews (Aka Surveys) Step 4

[ACTION STEP] (Add your responses to this exercise to your Reservoir of Information.)

HERE'S WHAT TO DO: I recommend that every online survey include ten questions or less and give a list of options. Why? Because open-ended questions in online surveys cause people to abandon the survey and not complete it.

Psychologically, open-ended surveys seem like too much work. But when you give people choices, you're making the path to completion easier.

As you rework the interview questions into survey questions with choices, consider these points:

- Write a summary paragraph to introduce the survey, set deadlines, and offer the giveaway.

- Use checkboxes over radio buttons to write *Check all that apply*.

- Include at least seven to ten checkbox options for each question.

- Use your ideal customer language whenever possible.

- Pull additional emotions and feelings into your choices.

- Alphabetize your options so the responses flow. It will make your question appear more polished and professional.

- Include an "Other" option for each question, so participants can write in additional comments that come to mind.

- Make each question mandatory.

- Write short, brief, targeted questions by using an active voice.

- Include a place for collecting the participant's email address so you have a way to contact each person. Collecting their email addresses also allow you to share survey results, distribute the promised thank you gift, and enter participants in the giveaway drawing.

To show you how your survey might look, I recently conducted the survey below on behalf of a Christian counseling group. I've lightly edited the survey to maintain client privacy.

Survey Example

Please use the following survey example as a guide, but do not copy it. You'll want to create your own survey to speak to your specific business and audience.

Survey Title: Help Us Help You

Summary/Intro Paragraph (at the top of the survey):

Hi there,

We'd appreciate your insights about how it feels to solve (the problem your audience was experiencing that your business solved). Would you take 90-seconds or less to answer these 10 questions and share your perspective?

As a thank you for sharing your insights by midnight Pacific Time US, February 25, 2021, you will receive access to our one-hour video—(insert name of the video)—that offers insights for (something their audience found valuable).

We will enter your name in a drawing for a $50 Amazon gift card.

The collective responses we receive will help us update our website and create new content to help (*description of their audience*)—just like you:

- o Strengthen and restore (*what their solutions achieve*)
- o Build (*something their solutions achieve*)
- o Recognize and break (*something their solutions achieve*)
- o and so much more.

We sincerely appreciate your thoughts.

With love and compassion,

(Client's Name)

If you wish to receive the free video and enter the $50 Amazon gift card drawing for participating in this survey, please provide your email in the space below.

```
┌──────────────────────────────────────────────┐
│                                                │
│                                                │
│                                                │
└──────────────────────────────────────────────┘
```

NOTE: The following questions mirror the questions that have been asked by phone. But these questions have a list of options. Each question is set up as "required," which means someone must answer every required question to participate in the survey. Each question had an alphabetized list of ten to fifteen possible responses plus one write-in box for comments labeled *Other*.

Survey Question Examples

What are the biggest frustrations you encounter in your (*description of target audience*)? (Check all that apply.)

```
┌──────────────────────────────────────────────┐
│  Insert an alphabetical list of options from   │
│  which to choose that you've heard your        │
│  customers talk about in your research and     │
│  interviews.                                    │
│                                                 │
└──────────────────────────────────────────────┘
```

What do you value most about your (*description of target audience*)? (Check all that apply.)

```
┌──────────────────────────────────────────────┐
│  Insert an alphabetical list of options from   │
│  which to choose that you've heard your        │
│  customers talk about in your research and     │
│  interviews.                                    │
│                                                 │
└──────────────────────────────────────────────┘
```

How does/did trying to solve your (*description of the problem*) issues make you feel? (Check all that apply.)

Insert an alphabetical list of options from which to choose that you've heard your customers talk about in your research and interviews.

What are the biggest things you've struggled with around building *(description of the problem they need to have solved)?* (Check all that apply.)

Insert an alphabetical list of options from which to choose that you've heard your customers talk about in your research and interviews.

If you could create a perfect *(description of the problem they need to have solved)*, what would it look like? (Check all that apply.)

Insert an alphabetical list of options from which to choose that you've heard your customers talk about in your research and interviews.

How would you feel if these problems didn't improve or you were in the same place a year from now? (Check all that apply.)

Insert an alphabetical list of options from which to choose that you've heard your customers talk about in your research and interviews.

How would you feel if these issues were no longer a problem for you? (Check all that apply.)

> Insert an alphabetical list of options from which to choose that you've heard your customers talk about in your research and interviews.

If you were going to recommend working with *(your business name)*, what would you say? (Please let us know if we share your recommendation online with your first name and last initial.)

> Make this open-ended so they can write in their response. *Note that this last question is open-ended and not required.*

Survey Email Examples

Survey Emails

The following examples are shared to give you an idea of what you might say. Please do not copy them. You'll want to customize them for your own business.

Email 1 to List

Target Audience:	Survey Email #1
From:	Your name
From Email:	Your email
Subject Line:	Need your advice, (first name)

Links:	To Google Forms, Typeform, or Survey Monkey

Hi, << First Name >>,

We need your advice.

You see, we're in the process of (state what you're doing, why, and how it will help clients).

Would you mind taking 90-seconds or less to answer ten quick questions?

Here's the link:

You will shape the types of information we share on our website and through our courses by weighing in.

To thank you for sharing your thoughts by **(insert date/time)**, we will enter your name in a drawing to win (insert really cool gift).

We sincerely appreciate your response.

Your standard signature close,

(Your Name)

Email 2 to List

Target Audience:	Survey Email #2
From:	Your name
From Email:	Your email
Subject Line:	Penny (or more) for your thoughts…
Links:	To Google Forms, Typeform, or Survey Monkey

Hi, << First Name >>,

I'm not sure if you saw the previous email we sent you.

But we sincerely want your input about the types of information you think would interest people who experience *(insert problem your audience has that your business solves).*

We designed the 10 questions to let you *weigh in by checking a few boxes.*

It should take you *less than 90-seconds* to do this.

In exchange for giving us your two cents by **(insert date)**, we'll enter your name in a drawing to win **(a really cool gift).**

And, of course, we'll be forever grateful for your time and thoughts.

Here's the link:

Thanks, in advance, for your guidance and input.

Your standard signature close,

(Your Name)

Email 3 to List

Target Audience:	Survey Email #3
From:	Your name
From Email:	Your email address
Subject Line:	Are you going to weigh in?
Links:	To Google Forms, Typeform, or Survey Monkey

Hi, << First Name >>,

Everyone has ideas and opinions...and we need yours.

If you've already filled out our quick survey, thank you for helping us.

If not, please take a moment to share your insights on building, restoring, and reviving family relationships.

We've made this simple:

Read through 10 questions.

Check a few boxes.

Click submit.

Here's the link:

When you do this before the end of the day **(insert date)**, you'll be entered into a drawing to **win one of two** *(really cool gifts).*

Someone has to win them, so it might as well be you. Right?!

The collective responses we receive will help us (restate what you're doing, why, and how it helps your audience achieve results.)

Who knows…you might find the new things we create interesting and helpful, too.

Thanks again for your help.

Your standard signature close,

(Your Name)

Email 4 to List

Target Audience:	Survey Email #4
From:	Your name
From Email:	Your email address
Subject Line:	Thank you, (first name)
Links:	none

Hi, << First Name >>,

Thank you for weighing in and giving us your thoughts.

The insights you shared are very helpful and will guide me as I continue to (problems your audience has that your business solves.)

Be on the lookout for the (promised valuable resource) that we're sending as a thank you.

In the interim, I'll leave you with this funny truth we saw and slightly modified:

Here's a list of the top 10 things to do when trying to grow connections and cultivate intimate relationships:

#1) Call (name of your business), and we'll show you how to handle the other 9.

Thanks again for your insights.

Your standard signature close,

(Your Name)

Compare Your Results to Your Perceptions

[ACTION STEP] (Add your responses to this exercise to your Reservoir of Information.)

HERE'S WHAT TO DO: After completing your SWOT analysis, interviews, and online surveys, you'll want to carve out time to review your results. Don't do this step on your own because you may overlook something without trying.

Ask your Business Partner, aka Abba Father, to help you see things through His eyes. Then systematically compare all the results to see what common themes jump out at you. You'll want to look for:

- Top problems your audience needs solved and opportunities they desire.

- Three to five of the top emotions your audience feels when they try to solve this issue.

- Three to five of the top emotions your audience feels when they achieve success.

- Areas you know your solutions will address.

- Things you feel led to address but don't yet.

- Patterns with common concerns, issues, and emotions that you need to elevate throughout your copy.

- Topics you could talk about and resolve through blog posts, lead magnets (aka giveaways you offer in exchange for email addresses), products, website copy, podcasts, webinars, etc.

- Objections your customers might have for what you're offering.

- Benefits your customers need to experience.

- Answers to the "reasons why" your solutions will help your customers do something, e.g., gain or save money, time, comfort, health, praise, or love.

Add a document of key findings to your Reservoir of Information that you will reference time and again as you address your audience's problems that your business solves. You will find that this research creates a wealth of information and insights that will serve you and your business well over time.

Don't consider the surveying and research a one-and-done project. Be intentional about strategically walking through these exercises with your audience and competitors in the future. WHY? Because needs, wants, and desires change when you least expect it.

After you compile your initial list, ask Holy Spirit to help you see which items you should elevate and focus on. Also, ask Him to point out topics you should avoid.

Just because an item surfaced on your list doesn't mean you're supposed to address it. Remember, your goal is to write joyful words that connect with your customers and authentically showcase where God wants you to shine the light.

25

MAPPING ESSENTIALS FOR YOUR SOLUTIONS

When you offer a product, service, or opportunity to a customer, you are—in basic terms—selling them a solution to an issue they need to have solved.

For example, a realtor helps homeowners find a property that meets their needs, wants, and desires for a place to live. Or a social media expert provides a business owner with strategy and tactical execution of social posts designed to build brand awareness, grow an audience, create engagement, and compel people to take action.

When you write about your solutions, you need to already know specific information about what you're offering.

This exercise may seem simple enough, but I've seen many people struggle with it because they haven't invested the time to develop a crystal clear vision of the specific details about their offerings.

As you get ready to do this product exercise, pause to ask Holy Spirit to help as you walk through the process. If you're not hearing Him, you may need to turn on praise and worship music. Invite the Lord into what you're doing and listen.

My friend Tasha Glover once asked me if I had ever laid prostrate on my face before the Lord. Her simple question was transformational in helping me hear Holy Spirit as I created materials for my business.

Since that time, if you could observe what goes on behind my closed office doors, you might see me lying on the floor with my hands out-stretched worshipping the Lord. You might also hear me praising God for all He has done, asking Him to guide me in what He would have me do, asking specific questions, and quietly listening.

The process I just described may seem strange to you at first. But I promise you that the Father WILL respond when you reach out to Him. Jeremiah 33:3 says: Call out Me, and I will show you incredible things that you do not know. And, boy, does He mean just that. Try it for yourself, and you'll see what I mean.

In this case, ask Abba to help you map out the solutions He wants you to offer.

Defining Products and Services Exercise Step 1

[ACTION STEP] (Add your responses to this exercise to your Reservoir of Information.)

HERE'S WHAT TO DO: For *each* product or service that you offer, you'll want to determine:

1. What problem does your product or service solve?

2. The features* that describe the facts about your product or service.

3. Specific benefits* for each product or service.

4. How your product works. (What features are included?)

5. Who uses this specific product or service?

6. What do prospective customers need to do to get this product or service?

7. What is the result your customers will experience when they use this product or service?

8. From beginning to end, describe the experience someone has when they use your product or service.

Before you dive into answering questions about your products, we need to spend a moment discussing the difference between features and benefits.

See Defining Products and Services Benefits Exercise Step 2

Features Tell. Benefits Sell.

This concept is difficult to grasp because the two terms—"features" and "benefits"—seem interchangeable. But they are not.

Features are FACTS about products and services. In comparison, benefits give someone a REASON to buy.

For example, in real estate, one feature might be A/C integrated throughout a property. But that is a fact, not a benefit.

You may be scratching your head, wondering how to turn that fact into a benefit. I'm so glad you asked.

When you list any feature, ask yourself, "So what?" about that feature.

Your answer will give you the benefit. In the case of the A/C, the answer to "so what?" is that the prospective homeowner will escape the heat and relax in the cool comfort of an air-conditioned home.

Let's look at a few more examples of turning features into benefits.

An oven preheats quickly. *So what?* The oven is quickly ready to start cooking your lasagna. *So what?* Your food is on the table faster. *So what?*

Life is less stressful because you spend less time in the kitchen waiting for your oven to get hot.

The *"so what?"* question will turn any feature into a benefit. You may need to ask the question several times until you drill down to the best answer. Here are additional examples showing how this process works.

- **Door Manufacturer** – Our doors have strong hinges. *So what?* They won't bend when the door is slammed shut a thousand times.

- **Network Service** – We monitor your servers. *So what?* Your servers won't go down, so you and your staff experience uninterrupted work time.

- **Marketer** – I develop content for businesses using proven techniques. *So what?* You'll increase your marketplace influence while providing prospects and customers valuable insights they can use.

Remember, your customers are in a hurry because they have a laundry list of competing priorities to accomplish. Depending on when they've stopped by your website or read your email, they may still need to write a blog post, catch up with the latest news, respond to a customer, or cook dinner.

Knowing your customer's situation is important because it is a good reminder that you have seconds to grab their attention while their cursor is hovering over the back button.

Let's walk through exactly how to help your features tell and benefits sell.

Defining Products and Services Benefits Exercise Step 2

[ACTION STEP] (Add your responses to this exercise to your Reservoir of Information.)

HERE'S WHAT TO DO: Pull out the features and benefits you wrote for each product or service. Drill down using the following five steps:

- Answer "so what?" about each feature.

- Make sure each benefit you previously wrote answers "so what?"

- Create a reason why the feature addresses your customer's need.

- Demonstrate what problem or pain point the feature solves, or hone in on the opportunity it creates.

- Ask Holy Spirit to give you His wisdom and discernment to see what you wouldn't otherwise have recognized about your benefits.

When the time is right, you'll pull from the answers about your products and services and weave it into the copy you write.

You must elevate benefits time and time again. Why? Because every human has an unspoken, ulterior motive—they want to know what's in it for me. (aka WIIFM)

Later on in this process, when you put everything together, you will:

- Highlight a key benefit (or problem your solution addresses) in your headlines or subheads.

- Use bullet points to list a series of features and benefits because they're easy to scan; mention the most important points first or last.

- Avoid using technical language (aka jargon) that your customer doesn't understand.

[ACTION STEP] Now would be a good time to go back and answer the questions about each of the products and services you currently sell or plan to sell in the marketplace. But don't do it in your own power or knowledge. Invite Abba Father to guide you.

As you write out your responses, keep reflecting on the biblical characteristics in the Ultimate How-To Guide. (You may also want to refer to the *Joyful Copy* Checklist included with this book.) Why? Because you want to make sure that what you're writing is genuine and true. You also want to make sure you aren't including any hype or manipulation in what you're offering.

Your Solution Won't...

Good copywriting addresses potential objections head-on. Seriously, good copywriting and salespeople know what objections a prospect might raise and strive to answer those questions before anyone even asks them.

If you want to write joyful copy, you will do the same thing. The only difference is your answer to the potential objections will always align with the teachings of the Bible. You will never answer with subtle hype or promises you never plan to fulfill.

You WILL remove potential roadblocks when you answer objections before a customer asks the question.

Think about God sending His Son to live on the earth, die for our sins, and rise from the dead. He did this to showcase His unconditional love. He also gave us His Son to overcome any objections we might have before we even raised the questions. Likewise, examples fill the Bible for every objection we might ever think of before we think of it. How cool is that?!

The purpose of uncovering objections in your business writing is to:

- Open doors
- Start conversations
- Close sales
- Help people
- Connect with customers
- Show you understand
- Meet their needs
- Demonstrate your value
- Guide people to solutions for their problems
- Shine His light to others
- And more.

So how do you determine objections in advance? I'm glad you asked.

While many books and tips are available about uncovering objections, I believe you need to focus on these four steps. But make sure you invite God into the process from the beginning.

Uncovering Objections Exercise

[ACTION STEP] (Add your responses to this exercise to your Reservoir of Information.)

HERE'S WHAT TO DO:

- Reflect on your business and what you sell or offer.

- Think about times someone has discussed working with you or a business like yours, then describe in written detail every one of the following that they have expressed.

  - Fear
  - Uncertainty
  - Emotion
  - Type of discomfort

- Write down every objection you've ever encountered or anticipate encountering about your business and specific products.

- After you've collected all the objections, describe why your business or service(s) resolves those objections.

  - Hint: Start by focusing on AT LEAST FIVE of the most common resolutions.

Now, go back and look at what you've written. Make sure you've captured what both a decision-maker and influencer might say. (When you're dealing with smaller businesses, the decision-maker and influencer might be one in the same person.)

If what you're offering is new, you'll need to interview people to ask hypothetical questions about what you will sell. Be sure to draw out any fears, uncertainties, emotions, or discomforts. Doing so will help you uncover potential objections you need to address.

It is important to note that every industry and niche will produce different objections.

The more knowledge you uncover about potential objections, the better prepared you'll be to address the concerns BEFORE someone mentions them.

As you write about your business, write open-ended questions about each objection and give your answers (reasons why) as your response (copy).

When you do this Uncovering Objections Exercise well, you will position yourself to increase the trust, likeability, and respect prospective customers have for and with you.

Why Will This Work for You?

My mom used to say that I was born asking questions and will still be asking questions after I'm buried six feet under. It's easy to hear the younger me saying, "But, why?"

From my perspective, the only way to learn is to ask questions. And I usually ask a bunch of them in every conversation. WHY? Because *information is power.*

When you write good copy about your business solutions, you will answer the why questions for your customers—answering why is just a different angle for overcoming objections.

WHY do you want to answer WHY? Because answering why will give your audience reasons to read, engage, and buy when the time is right for them. Notice I didn't say that answering why will magically get people to buy even when they don't need whatever you're selling.

When you're writing joyful copy, you will give all the information someone needs to take a specific action, but you'll leave the timing of making that decision up to them. If you align your marketing copywriting with Bible teachings, God will use your words to penetrate hearts and minds. I firmly believe He will also bring your copy to mind and help people think of you when the time is right for them.

Here are some verses for you to ponder as you work through this:

Every single activity in life has a season and time to happen. (~Ecclesiastes 3:1, Joy's Paraphrase)

Planning is good, but realize God will have the last word. (~Proverbs 16:1, Joy's Paraphrase)

Like most topics, the Bible has a LOT to say about reasoning.

As a Christ-following entrepreneur, you need to think about your audience, their whys, and how you can address them. Pray about reasons you may offer your audience to participate, partner, buy, take action, etc.

Remember, while you're doing these exercises in partnership with God by seeking His guidance, you're sharing your work with people from all walks of life. Some may have a deep, personal relationship with God. Others may know Him but only on the surface at a ritualistic level. And still others may not care about anything to do with God.

Regardless of someone's beliefs and values, it is important to show your customers and prospects WHY you do what you do and how it will genuinely help them. So make sure you take time to write out an answer for every WHY that will speak to your ideal customers.

Master copywriter Jim Edwards teaches that it is important to include more than one reason why in your copy. According to Jim's extensive body of knowledge, he encourages answering ten reasons why for every item you sell. I've modified his list to five points that pull out basic human needs most people strive to achieve.

Like everything else, before you dive into the WHY Exercise, I want to encourage you to ask Holy Spirit to guide you to hear and see the way He hears and sees.

Give Them a Reason: The Answer Why Exercise

[ACTION STEP] (Add your responses to this exercise to your Reservoir of Information.)

HERE'S WHAT TO DO: Think outside the box and try to write at least five reasons why for every product or service you sell. Answer why your solutions will help these basic human needs happen:

- make and save money
- avoid pain and gain comfort
- improve health
- feel loved or praised
- save time and effort

The answers to these questions will add to your reservoir of information. You'll weave these reasons into your offers, headlines, stories, and calls to action.

Once you understand your whys, you'll also want to pull out and elevate points your competitors don't mention. In turn, it will help your business stand out in the marketplace.

[Ongoing Action Step] (Journal Your Responses)

HERE'S WHAT TO DO: Once again, you'll want to run everything you're uncovering and planning to share with your audience through your Business Partner to make sure what you're planning to say fits into His design for your business. You'll also want to ensure what you share is in complete alignment with the teachings of the Bible without twisting reality to get people to act.

Determine Your God-Given Gifts and Talents

The common phrase you may have heard used in marketing is USP (aka Unique Selling Proposition). While determining how your business is different from others is important, I like to put the USP on its side and look at it through God's lens. I call this determining your God-given gifts and talents.

Since we are uniquely made and not called to imitate each other, I encourage you to find out what gifts God gave you to use in the marketplace (Psalm 139:13–14).

Darren Shearer wrote a book with exercises that will help you drill down into your spiritual gifts. I highly recommend reading his materials and taking the quizzes, so check out *The MarketPlace Christian*.

While there are definite spiritual gifts in the Bible, I am talking about the God-given gifts and talents that extend *beyond* the spiritual gifts.

If you have a gift for teaching, selling, coaching, leading, technology, problem-solving, baking, speaking, finances, project management, diagnosing and healing with medicine, educating, etc., THOSE gifts are also God-given.

Our Ultimate How-To Guide has a lot to say about talents. Let me share a few examples:

God created you to do good works. He planned out what He wanted you to do before He created you in your mother's womb. (~Ephesians 2:10, Joy's Paraphrase)

Everyone is to use their skills and talents to create what God needs and has asked them to do. Be obedient. (~Exodus 35:10, Joy's Paraphrase)

God is responsible for sending every good gift your way. He is the Creator of all things who remains constant and never varies. (~I James 1:17, Joy's Paraphrase)

Let's take inventory. The next exercises will help you determine your God-given gifts and talents to hone your messages about what God has called you to offer in the marketplace. You will weave both into what you write and say about your business.

Wave Your Freak Flag

Everywhere we look today, people love to "wave their freak flag" and show how they are different from the norm. You need to do the same thing in business by showcasing your God-given gifts and talents to tell why someone should tap into your solutions.

From today's marketplace perspective, you may recognize some of these USP examples:

- Pizza delivered in thirty minutes or it's free. (Domino's Pizza)

- When it absolutely, positively has to be there overnight. (FedEx)

- A round of golf in four hours or less or your next green fee is on us. (Rolling Hills Country Club)

- If any Craftsman hand tool fails to provide complete satisfaction, return it for free repair or replacement. Period. The first Craftsman hand tool we sold back in 1927 is still under warranty today. (Craftsman Tools)

- The best return policy ever. A return policy that removes the fear of buying online and buying shoes that might not fit. (Zappos)

- Dropbox keeps your files safe, synced, and easy to share. Bring your photos, docs, and videos anywhere, and never lose a file again. (Dropbox)

From a faith-based perspective, you may recognize some of these God-given gifts examples. (Note: I captured these examples over time, and each one may have shifted with the entrepreneur as God shifted them.)

- Experience God's best in your business and have a greater kingdom impact in the marketplace. (Kingdom-Driven Entrepreneur)

- Identity Aligned Success: Christian CEO (Kelly Baader)
- Stronger faith. More profits. Real impact.
  - Prosper from your gifts. (Althea McIntyre)
- My Passions:
  - Writing words you've been needing.
  - Teaching Biblical Truth You've Been Looking For.
  - Uncomplicating therapy so you can find healing.
  - Helping other writers fulfill their dreams.
  - Leading people to Jesus through Proverbs 31 Ministries (Lysa Terkeurst)
- Building thriving marriages and successful businesses
  - End the power struggle between your marriage and business. Power Couples by Design will help you resolve:
    - Financial stress
    - Poor communication issues
    - Inconsistent profitability
    - Work-life-play balance (~i61, Inc. - Power Couples by Design)
- Restoring personal connections and communications—one relationship at a time (The Family Collective)

Now, it's your turn to uncover and use your God-given gifts and talents in the copy about your business.

Even if your business isn't faith-based, this exercise still applies to what you do. It is essential to partner with Holy Spirit to determine what gifts He wants you to elevate. Since He IS the Creator who made you, He will give you better insights than any human ever could about what unique elements you should elevate through your business.

Your God-Given Gifts Exercise Step 1

[ACTION ITEM] (Add your responses to this exercise to your Reservoir of Information.)

HERE'S WHAT TO DO:

1. Start by sitting with the Lord and asking Him to reveal any gift and talents that He wants you to elevate about yourself and your business. Don't be surprised if gifts and talents you didn't know you had come to mind. You may even think of gifts and talents you haven't used in a while.

2. Review your SWOT analyses to look for:

   ○ Gifts you or your business have that your competitors may not possess

   ○ Differentiators you both possess, but you may deliver in a different way

3. Look at your Reservoir of Information to extract answers to these questions:

   ○ What do you offer that your competitors don't?
   ○ Is this important to your customers? Why?
   ○ What problem does this differentiator solve, if any?
   ○ Can you describe it easily?

Your God-Given Gifts Exercise Step 2

[ACTION ITEM] (Add your responses to this exercise to your Reservoir of Information.)

HERE'S WHAT TO DO:

1. Choose one or more of the frameworks below.

2. Write out at least five (or more) versions of the frameworks below and make them your own.

- Don't mention your products.

- Don't get caught up in semantics.

- Don't overthink this.

- Be factual, simple, and clear.

- Don't embellish, but don't be vague.

- Make sure you can back up what you say/write.

- Focus on the problems you solve/opportunities you offer and how your God-given gifts and talents help you solve them differently than others.

- Test what you write on others so it makes sense to "Joe Q. Public."

- Keep tweaking until you find the right combination of concise and easily understood words.

Before you select any framework, let's walk through Message Framework ONE with a bit of additional explanation and an example of a framework filled out.

Notice the arrows with call out boxes are used to provide explanation of what you'll want to put in that blank.

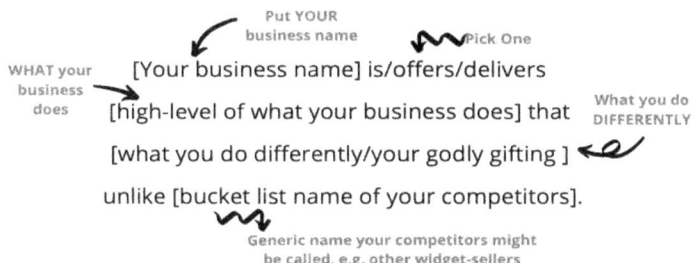

Notice that I highlighted and bolded the copy I was inserting to make clear what section was filled in. When you use a framework, you would remove the brackets.

[Engaging Business Communications] offers
[joyful copywriting and values-based business coaching]
that **[aligns with the teachings of the Bible]**
unlike **[some marketers]**.

Messaging Framework One:

[Your business name] is/offers/delivers [high-level of what your business does] that [what you do differently/your godly gifting] unlike [bucket list name of your competitors]

Messaging Framework Two:

I understand [customer's problem that you solve], so I was led to create [your offering] that [explain what you do differently/your godly gifting]

Messaging Framework Three:

[Your Ideal Customer] to [experience this desired result] for [this specific benefit]

Messaging Framework Four:

[Top Problem/Desired Opportunity/Result]

[Because of these Points of Difference]

Put what you write into your Reservoir of Information as you'll pull from it when you write various pieces of content in future *Joyful Copy* lessons and when you write about your business.

Honing Your Message

When someone connects with you in an elevator, online, or in passing, you have just a few moments to capture their attention and make a connection. Since you never know where a passing interaction might lead, it is wise to prepare what you want to say about your business so it flows easily and conversationally. When people ask you what you do, you need to have the words ready to share.

Think back to meetings and interactions where someone rambles on without getting to the point. Once they finally conclude, you're exhausted, disconnected, and ready to move on to the next item. Does that sound familiar?! I know, I've been there, too.

Don't wait until those moments happen. Prepare in advance. Use this time to nail down the details of your message to easily answer the question, "What do you do?"

Here's the good news: You'll also use this messaging exercise on your website and throughout the content you create, so be sure to save it in your Reservoir of Information.

Your goal is to write out the following:

1. Who do you serve?
2. What value do you provide?
3. What problems do you solve, or what opportunities do you offer?
4. How do you deliver these solutions or opportunities?
5. Why should a prospective customer do business with you?
6. How are you and your God-given gifts different than others?

While your message is NOT a slogan or positioning statement, it should be to the point, using as few words as possible. Ideally, in just a few seconds, you should be able to say it, and your customers should be able to scan it.

To write this statement well, you need to do the following:

- Research your audience.
- Create an ideal customer profile.
- Research your competitors.
- Determine the primary benefits of what you do and HOW your God-given gifts help you do it differently than others.

Your God-Given Message Exercise

[ACTION ITEM] (Add your responses to this exercise to your Reservoir of Information.)

HERE'S WHAT TO DO:

1. Choose one or more of the following frameworks. (See below)
2. Write out at least five versions of each type.
   - Don't get caught up in semantics.
   - Be factual. Don't embellish.
   - Focus on your customers' issues and how you solve them.
   - You want what you write to make sense to "joe public."
   - Use common terminology that someone might use as search terms on Google to find what you offer.

After You Write

1. Read through what you've written.
2. Pray over what you write.
3. Tweak what you've written as you feel led.
4. Select your best messages for possible use later.

Before you select any framework, let's walk through God-Given Framework TWO with a bit of additional explanation and an example of a framework filled out.

Notice the arrows with call out boxes are used to provide explanation of what you'll want to put in that blank.

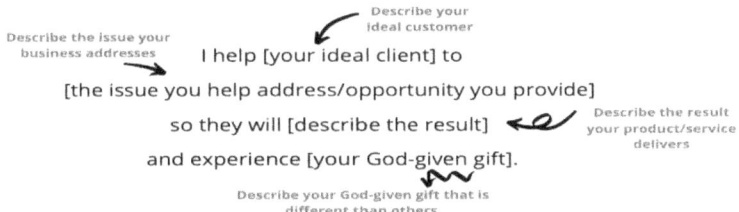

Notice that I highlighted and bolded the copy I was inserting to make clear what section was filled in. When you use a framework, you would remove the brackets.

For [Christ-following entrepreneurs] to

[learn how to write joyful copy]

so they will [connect with customers authentically]

and experience [God's supernatural transformation].

Your God-Given Message Framework One:

For [ideal customer] who [need/desire] our [product/service/opportunity] will [benefit or result] from our [God-Given gift].

Your God-Given Message Framework Two:

I help [describe your ideal client] to [the issue you help address/opportunity you provide] so they will [describe the result] and experience [your God-given gift].

Your God-Given Message Framework Three:

> I help [ideal client] experience [result you promise] and [God-given gift] by [action word] the [your product, service, solution].

Before you write, ask the Lord to guide you. Once you've written out several examples of each framework, complete each step below:

- Ask Holy Spirit to help you refine your message.
- Test your messages by sharing them with others.
- Ask if what you shared is easy to understand.
- Select your best versions and practice saying them aloud.
- Memorize them so you're ready to communicate quickly and easily when an opportunity arises.
- Put the top critical messages into your Reservoir of Information so you can weave them into copy for your marketing as needed.

Once you've honed your message, it is time to collect some social proof. Let's look at how to do this in the next section.

Collecting and Using Testimonials

Testimonials provide social proof for what your business offers. What people have to say about your business is a core component you need to share with the world.

If you think about the ministry of Jesus and His disciples, they had testimonies about their work that traveled quickly by word of mouth. As the years went by, what was said about them was captured in the scriptures for everyone to read throughout the centuries.

Today, you'll find testimonials, reviews, and endorsements in various places online or in print. Capturing and sharing what others have to say about a business, product, or service gives credibility beyond what you say. The thoughts of others can strengthen (or tear down) easily.

When you go to some websites, you'll notice a dedicated testimonial page when you go to some websites. While there is nothing wrong with that approach, I recommend seizing every opportunity to share what your customers say in the moment.

You do this by weaving testimonials into every sales page and web page. Whenever it makes sense, share a soundbite endorsement. Just make sure to balance it with your message so the reader's eyes don't begin to glaze over from too much of a good thing.

Don't make people stop what they are doing to look up what others say. Just like answering objections before people bring them up, you'll want to offer recommendations early and often.

The best way to collect testimonials is to *ask for them*. I firmly believe in the "you have not because you asked not" philosophy (James 4:2–3).

From day one, when you help someone for free, test your product or service in the marketplace, or sell your first course--you need to ask for testimonials.

I believe in this so strongly that I include a clause in my contracts where my clients agree to provide testimonials.

Why is this important? Because true testimonials build trust, credibility, and social proof.

How to Ask for Testimonials

What should you ask? You may want to use this simple questionnaire that I share with customers.

Testimonials Exercise

[ACTION ITEM] (Add the responses you collect from this exercise to your Reservoir of Information.)

HERE'S WHAT TO DO: Ask customers if they will give you a testimonial. Once they agree, follow up with an email that includes your own variation of the following email copy. (While you are welcome to copy the email below word for word, I encourage you to make it your own.)

> Hi, {Client Name},
>
> Thank you for agreeing to share your feedback about working with me (or business/product name if you're asking this on behalf of a business or product).
>
> Would you kindly answer the following questions? Don't worry about wordsmithing. I'll edit it for you.
>
> - What did you work on with (name of person or business)?
> - What was your biggest challenge BEFORE working with (her/him/them)?
> - How did the challenge you were experiencing make you feel?
> - What results did you experience from working with (her/him/them)?
> - What would you tell someone about what it is like to work with (name of person or business)?
>
> Thank you for your time.
>
> {Your Name}

You may have to follow up a few times before people respond. One way to nudge people to completion from the beginning is to offer a discount or gift (similar to the survey gifts) that you'll send them as soon as you hear back from them.

Like every section before, you'll want to pray about WHO you ask for testimonials. Then ask Holy Spirit to help you use those endorsements wisely at the right time and place.

Finally, put the testimonials you collect into your Reservoir of Information as you'll pull from it when you write various pieces of content in future lessons and for your business.

If you have the resources, kick it up a notch by asking for video testimonials. An easy way to do this is by asking people to record a Loom video and send you the link. If you're not familiar with Loom, you can check it out at www.loom.com.

PART V
REFLECTION QUESTIONS

As we're wrapping up this book, I want to encourage you to continue spending time working through these reflection questions before moving forward. Journaling your responses will give you points in time to reflect on later to ascertain how much you've grown.

Points to Ponder

When you work on your business, what percentage of time do you try to do it on your own? What percentage of time do you seek the Lord's guidance?

What steps can you take to create a true partnership with God in your business and marketing?

What questions do you need to ask Abba Father about your business? Write them down. Ask Him your questions, then listen and take action on what you hear.

Whose voice do you hear as you work on your business? Write down your thoughts, both negative and positive. Cross out the negative ones, which are not from God. Circle the positive ones. Then pray for God to help you stay focused on His voice, and bind the powers of Satan in Jesus' name around the negative ones.

What does Holy Spirit want you to elevate and focus on in your business? What topics do you think He's leading you to avoid?

PART VI: DISTILL *JOYFUL COPY:* CONNECTING WITH YOUR CUSTOMERS

Now that you've gathered information about your customers, competitors, and what God wants you to do in and through your business, you should have compiled a solid *Reservoir of Information*. Now it is time to learn some basic copywriting skills and build out some content.

In this section, we'll explore:

- WHO to focus on
- Active versus Passive Writing
- What to Do Before You Write
- How to Create and Use Joyful Headlines
- What to Do After You Write

Let's start by talking about WHO to focus on when you write.

26

IT'S ALL ABOUT YOU!

N ow don't get too excited. I'm **not** saying you want to focus on yourself and your products whenever you write—just the opposite. The harsh reality is that we live in a me-centric world where most people care only about themselves. So, the first copywriting tip to remember when you write is to emphasize "YOU" (aka your audience).

I've tried to model this concept throughout this book by writing to you as if we were sitting down over a cup of coffee. Go back and flip through the pages, and you'll notice the word "you" is prevalent in what I've written. WHY? *Because you draw people in by focusing on them first.* It's NOT about YOU. It's about THEM.

Some of the concepts in this chapter may sound familiar because we touched on them in Chapter 6 when we talked about heartfelt joy as a fruit of the Spirit. Here, I'm describing both a copywriting technique and a biblical principle (Matthew 6:33 and Philippians 2:3–4). While God's Word makes it clear that you are amazing and incredible, Scripture also teaches that you should *put God first, then focus on others and yourself last.*

When you put yourself last, you WILL stand out because everyone else is me-centric and copying what they see others do. People put themselves first all the time, whether they admit it or not.

Remember how I shared that my mom has modeled how to put others first throughout my life. She still does it to this day. When she does that, Mom becomes memorable instantly. For example, right before the lockdown for the pandemic, my daddy passed away. Mom was left by herself on a remote island off the coast of Southwest Florida with no human interaction. (Yes, I know we were all walking through that in different ways, but stick with me for a second more.)

Since my mom is an outgoing, do-for-others person, she found a way to still connect with people. She would quietly walk alone around the neighborhood at night to get outside and exercise. As she walked, she would leave notes of encouragement in the mailboxes of each of her neighbors. Do you think that action made her memorable? You bet. Was she talking about herself and sharing how awesome she was with anyone who would listen? Nope. In fact, a lot of what she did was anonymous. After a while, it was easy for people to realize that Patsy (that's my mom's name) was the encourager. Talk about putting others first and standing out in a crowd.

I share this point to illustrate the power of putting those you are trying to connect with before yourself. Just remember the JOY acronym (**JOY = Jesus First, Others Second, Yourself Last**) when you talk, create, and write, and you'll be set. Living life according to the teachings of the Bible AND good copywriting uses JOY.

Make Instant Connections

To illustrate the power of YOU further, pause to think about your last conversation with someone that felt like an instant connection. Why did that happen? Because immediate rapport occurs whenever you talk about what's important to another person.

Don't believe me? Test it out. While you're having a conversation with someone who is focusing on himself, try switching the topic to something else. Try to talk about yourself or one of your projects.

Unless what you share helps that person solve a problem or is a topic to which he can relate, he will probably zone out. Sure, the person may humor you for a few moments to be polite, but he won't stick to the new topic you've presented for long.

Nine times out of ten, you'll see the person's eyes glaze over, and he will check out of the conversation. Change the topic back to him or something he is interested in, and he will magically reengage like a veil has been lifted. You are guaranteed to get someone's attention the minute you start talking about that person's problems, wants, desires, or needs.

Think about the last "must-have" product or program you knew you must buy. Everything written about that product focused on YOU…your problems, your wants, your (fill in the blank) that you needed to solve.

It makes us all sound very selfish, but our innate desire to focus on ourselves is a fact of life. Since self-focus is human nature, you might benefit from learning how to use this intel in your communications effectively.

How to Use YOU in Copy

Are you wondering how you'll apply this concept to what you write about your business? Follow these steps when you write.

[ACTION STEP] (Tab this section so you can refer to it easily or add this list to your Reservoir of Information.)

HERE'S WHAT TO DO: Follow these tips when you write.

- Pique interest and draw in customers by turning "we" into "you."

- Use the language of your customers.

- Put the spotlight on **their** problems, wants, and desires (that your solutions solve.)

- Show you understand what's important to **them.**

- Share relatable stories with which they can connect easily.

- Then—when the time is right—bring up the amazing, transformative solutions you offer.

- Tell them what to do next to get your solution, download something for free, sign up for a webinar, etc.

Whatever you write, focus on THEM, not YOU. You'll experience results when you apply JOY to all you do. (No pun intended.)

27

SHE WRITES *JOYFUL COPY* (ACTIVE VS. PASSIVE)

Writing good copy also uses active voice, not passive voice. While writing in an active voice is a toe-stubber to many, it is important because doing so will make what you write stronger. Many self-proclaimed "grammar nazis" consider passive voice weak and timid.

Now, don't get me wrong. Sometimes, you simply can't avoid passive voice. But, as a rule of thumb, try to write sentences where your subject takes action.

Writing with an active voice uses few words to make what you write more concise and easier to understand. Active voice will also make your tone more conversational, which is another key to writing engaging copy that connects with your audience.

To make sure we're on the same page, I want to encourage you to take a look at this chart with Active-Passive Examples.

Active Voice	Passive Voice
[Thing doing action] + [verb] + [thing receiving action].	[Thing receiving action] + [be] + [past participle of verb] + [by] + [thing doing action].
I love him.	I am loved by him.
I write an email.	An email is written by me.
He buys a camera.	A camera is bought by him.
Water fills a tub.	A tub is filled with water.
He will hire new team members.	New team workers were hired by him.
She will release new content.	The new content will be released.
They know me.	I am known to them.

If you're like me, you may pause to look up what the Bible has to say about passive and active voice. While you'll find many fascinating opinions, and Scripture uses both voices from cover to cover, remember that God's Word is full of verses about taking action.

Here's my paraphrase of a few verses that address the need to take action instead of passively waiting for something to happen.

- Colossians 3:23–24: Whatever task you have to do, do your best.

- Luke 11:9: Keeping asking, seeking, and knocking for God's will in all you do.

- James 4:17: Knowing what is right to do and not doing it is a sin.

- 1 Peter 1:13: Prepare your mind for action, be self-disciplined, and fix your hope on God.

- James 1:22: Show up, take action, and do more than listen to God's Word. Ignore anything that runs contrary to God's Word.

When it comes to shining God's light in the world, you *need* to take action. Likewise, follow what the Ultimate How-To Guide models by writing copy using active voice.

Next, let's roll up your sleeves and dig into what to do BEFORE you write.

28

FIRE, READY, AIM

Imagine that you're sitting at your desk when the phone rings. The person on the line shares that you've moved up on the waitlist, and an opening is available for the meeting you requested months ago. But there's one caveat: you need to arrive before the end of the day.

You know your destination is about six hours away in another state, but that doesn't stop you. Without pausing to think, you grab a few items, hop in the car, and head to the airport.

You don't do any prep work before you walk out the door. You don't check to make sure you have the files you need on your laptop. You don't make any travel arrangements or pack an overnight bag. You just grab your keys and go.

Once you get to the airport, you buy the first available—yet over-priced—flight and hope for the best. Your enthusiasm is in the driver's seat, propelling you forward. Adrenaline is fueling your excitement.

You're taking action without thinking the situation through completely, but this approach is how you live life. And let's face it, sometimes it works out. But at other times…well, not so much.

So, how do you think that meeting will turn out? Maybe you know the outcome because you've been in that exact situation in the past.

Now, what if that same scenario played out, but this time you paused long enough to get your ducks in a row before running out the door? What if you methodically checked available flights and created a checklist to make the meeting a success? The meeting is certain to generate better results. Right?!

It is a fact that most endeavors in life and business will work out a bit smoother when you have a game plan in place. Sure, you'll have to pivot and change along the way at times, but nine times out of ten you'll achieve success when you figure out where you're going and how you'll get there *before* you embark on your journey.

No matter the task—from product development to meetings to shopping to weight loss to cooking—you'll get where you're going faster and easier if you plan your trip before you go.

Plan Before You Take Action

Any business trip, phone conference, or even a simple trip to the grocery store will have better results when you map out a plan beforehand. The same applies to writing copy. Before you write any words to build awareness or promote your solutions, you need to start with the end in mind.

Before You Write Exercise Step 1

[ACTION STEP] (Tuck this insight into your mind. Add it to your Reservoir of Information if it helps you remember: *Ask God first.*)

HERE'S WHAT TO DO: Before you map everything out, you'll want to spend time with Your Business Partner, asking Him to guide you through the planning process.

Since God's Word has a LOT to say about planning in concert with Him, you'll undoubtedly experience greater success when you invite Holy Spirit into the process at the very beginning. Note that I didn't say invite Him into the process to bless something AFTER you've already created it.

Let's peek at some of the verses that support our living, loving God's desire to guide and direct your work. He makes His desire clear.

- Come near to God, and He will come near to you. (James 4:8a)

- Suppose one of you wants to build a tower. Won't you first sit down and estimate the cost to see if you have enough money to complete it? (Luke 14:28)

- Commit to the Lord whatever you do, and he will establish your plans. (Proverbs 16:3)

- In their hearts, humans plan their course, but the Lord establishes their steps. (Proverbs 16:9)

An old hymn written in 1855 sweetly shares how Jesus is there waiting to help you through any and every situation. "What a friend we have in Jesus, all our sins and griefs to bear. What a privilege to carry *everything* to God in prayer."

The message is clear throughout Scripture, in hymns, and hopefully in this book: We should not compartmentalize God to once-a-week Saturday or Sunday rituals. We should turn to Him throughout *every* aspect of our lives and business, from the moment we get up to the moment we go to sleep. He wants to partner with us.

He is ready to help you with *everything*—you need only call out to Him, listen, and respond.

Once you've invited Him into what you're doing, you're ready to start planning.

Before You Write Exercise Step 2

[ACTION STEP] (Tuck this insight into your mind. Add it to your Reservoir of Information if it helps you remember: *Start with the end in mind.*)

HERE'S WHAT TO DO: Just like you plan a trip before you depart, you'll want to take time to answer these questions BEFORE you write. (We go over this again in the last chapter.

- **WHO** – Who is your audience for what you're creating and writing?

    o What are their likes and dislikes?
    o What are their needs, wants, and desires?

- **WHAT** – What are you writing?

    o Are you writing a webpage? An email campaign? A landing page? A sales page? A product roadmap or workshop? A blog?

- **GOAL** – What is the purpose of what you're writing?

    o Are you trying to educate or inform about a particular topic? Perhaps you want to persuade the reader to your way of thinking.
    o Do you have a specific product or service to sell?
    o Are you writing to engage your audience and build trust?

When you determine the purpose and intent for your copy, you will know what to focus on in your writing. But don't paint a one-size-fits-all picture with your words. Be very specific and try to focus on one thing at a time.

- **ONE** – Since a confused mind never buys, you want to focus on one thing at a time.

    o   Is there ONE big idea or story you could use to make your point?
    o   What are the key points of that ONE thread?
    o   Hone in on **one idea** that plays on **one emotion** and offers **one key benefit** to your reader.

- **REASONABLE ACTION** – Many writers tell people WHAT to do, but they forget to tell them WHY they should do it. Good copy has a clear goal that leads to a specific action. Better copy will also include a reason WHY someone needs to take action. Be sure to determine and specify these two points.

    o   What specific action do you want your reader to take?
    o   Why should someone take that action?

If you want your readers to Buy Now, Learn More, Join Free for 30 Days, Sign Up Now, Read More, or Get Free Updates— you need to be clear, action-oriented, and "ask for the sale."

Tell readers what to do and motivate them to do so by giving them reasons why that action will resonate with their needs.

- **PROOF** – Power comes from results and what others say about their experience. Make sure you include:

    o   One-to two-sentence quote or testimonial to validate what you're saying.
    o   Data points and/or statistics that demonstrate results.

On each of these items that you map out, make sure what you plan to write and include is authentic, genuine, and aligns with the teachings of the Bible.

Now that you have your plan outlined, you need to create a structure for what you'll write. The best way to do this is by writing headlines and subheads for the copy you're creating.

29

MADE YOU LOOK: THE SECRET TO WRITING JOYFUL HEADLINES

One of the first steps in writing good copy involves writing headlines. WHY? Because headlines will draw in readers, break up your copy, and cater to the scanners of today's online world.

Headlines also form the structure of what you'll write, just like the frame forms the structure of a house. An architect draws up plans that the builder uses to frame a home, then the house is built around that frame. Headlines are similar to the frame of a house. They will give the copy you've planned some structure to make sure everything fits well together.

Early on, you read how powerful headlines are for grabbing attention and getting people to read what you've written. You may recall that many use clickbait to pull the wool over people's eyes, but that approach doesn't align with God's Word.

Writing Headlines Exercises

[ACTION STEP] (Tab this section so you can refer to the headline tips and frameworks easily. Add the headlines you create to your Reservoir of Information.)

HERE'S WHAT TO DO: Writing good headlines is considered an art by many. But writing good headlines that possess Joyful Alignment is a God thing. It is easy when you know what to do.

The following pages contain some frameworks that, when used correctly, will work to engage your audience without twisting reality, creating hype, or using manipulation.

A few things to note:

- **Find Examples** – Headline frameworks are a dime a dozen. You can find examples of headlines everywhere you look. And at the end of this section, I'll tell you where to look for more ideas.

- **Use *Your* Words** – When you find a headline framework you like, make it your own, so the words speak to your audience's needs. Do NOT copy a headline you see word for word unless you have permission from the person who wrote it.

- **Practice Makes Perfect** – The first thing you write probably won't be your best work. Write out at least five different examples of each framework. Then pick the best one for the piece you're working on.

- **Be Authentic and Sincere** – Make sure what you write doesn't twist reality to get people to take action.

- **Seek Wisdom** – Talk to Abba Father about what you plan to write and ask for His guidance. Then talk to Him about what you've written and ask Him to help you see it through His eyes.

- **Filter Through Frameworks** – After you've written your copy and before you share it with the world, filter your copy through at least three core frameworks. (We'll walk through some core frameworks I recommend using after we talk about headlines.)

Let's walk through each example and look at when you might apply that type of headline and how to keep it joyful.

How-to Headline Frameworks

Everyone loves to learn how to do something, improve, or fill a need. Use the how-to headline to evoke curiosity and provide helpful tips. The options for this type of headline are endless.

Joyful Copy Alignment: List only benefits for which you can offer actual guidance and insights toward achieving. If you don't know how to teach or coach these benefits, your headline is not Joyfully Aligned.

- How-to (Action/Product) + (Action/Goal)
- How to (List Benefit) and (List Benefit)
- How to Win Friends and Influence People (Dale Carnegie)
- How to Get a Better Job and Make More Money (Recruiter)
- How to Use Social Media to Get Lead
- How I Learned to Wake Up Refreshed Every Morning
- How to Define Your Ideal Customer
- How to (_____) in as little as (_____)...even if you (_____)
- How everyone (_____) can (_____)
- How to...Get, Have, Start, Keep, Become, Improve, End, Avoid

Question Headline Frameworks

Asking a burning question already on your reader's mind will create a connection that finds your customer leaning in. WHY? Questions evoke curiosity because everyone is searching for answers.

Joyful Copy Alignment: Avoid yes or no questions because that will stop the conversation before it starts. Ask only open-ended questions which you know interest your audience, and you can answer successfully. You don't want to create a false sense of curiosity or desire using the question headline.

- Do You Know How to (_____)?
- What's the Secret of (_____)?
- Are You Paying Too Much for (_____)?
- Who Else Wants to (_____)?
- What Would Happen If You (_____)?
- Are You (_____)?
- Do You Really Need (_____)?

Inside Knowledge Headline Frameworks

Use insider knowledge as a benefit for your readers. This well-used formula works well for genuine experts.

Joyful Copy Alignment: Only allude to insider tips if the information is something you know your readers will benefit from learning and you sincerely know information about the topic. If it is common knowledge and you're just trying to bring readers to a sale, you need to pause and rethink your strategy; what you're trying to do probably doesn't align with your Ultimate How-To Guide.

- The Secret of/to (_____)
- The Secret of the Hidden Scrolls
- The Secret to Sleeping Well Without Medication
- The Secret of Making People Like You

- (#) Little-Known Facts about (_____)
- (#) Secrets of Successful (_____)
- What (_____) Will Teach You about (_____)
- What (_____) Should Know about (_____)
- The Truth about (_____)

Remember, smaller numbers draw people because it seems more realistic and easy to digest, while larger numbers may seem a bit daunting and overwhelming. For example, Five Little-Known Facts about Scuba Diving is more appealing than 115 Little-Known Facts about Scuba Diving.

If you use a larger number, you'll want to make sure the content is compelling and interesting enough that people will finish reading whatever you share.

Transaction Headline Frameworks

The exchange headline asks for something and then offers to give something in return. You'll use this type of headline for reciprocity.

Joyful Copy Alignment:

- Use this type of headline only if you can follow through on your promise.

- Remember, we are called to let our "yes" be "yes" and our "no" be "no," including following through on every promise we make.

- Don't be like many who make bold promises they never intend to keep just to get the reader to take action.

Here are some frameworks to try:

- Give me (valuable thing), and I'll give you (promise of more)
- Try these (valuable things), and you'll be (promise)

- (#) quick and easy ways to (_____)
- (#) fast ways to get (_____) and avoid (_____)

Get What You Want Headline Frameworks

Your audience already has desires and/or specific goals they want to achieve. Use this headline to help people achieve a specific goal.

When you dig deep, you'll see there is more to acquire or achieve than money. Sadly, when you look around, you see many entrepreneurs focus mainly on making money. Remember that while money is good, it is not the end-all and be-all because God has so much more planned for those who genuinely seek Him.

Let me encourage you to dig deep into the needs of your audience to uncover goals besides money that you can help them reach.

Joyful Copy Alignment: Offer the end result only within a given time period. Just make sure that what you are offering is indeed possible. For example, if you tell people they will lose thirty pounds in six months using your solution, make sure you're able to deliver on that promise.

- Lose 10 Lbs. in 30 Days without Exercise
- Sell More Homes in One Quarter by Following These Steps
- Get Immediate Workers' Comp Quotes Now *(Creates a sense of urgency because you're getting quotes when? Now!)*
- (End Result) + (Time Period) + (Objective)
- (#) Money-/Time-Saving Tips for (_____)
- How to Find the Best (_____) Deals on the Web
- Top Gadgets to Help You (_____)
- Everything You Need to Know about Getting (_____)

Reason Why Headline Frameworks

Tap into curiosity and draw your reader in by offering to answer WHY about something that interests your audience. Think back to "The Answer Why Exercise" you completed in Chapter 18.

Studies show that people are drawn to lists, so add more spice to your why headline by adding the number of reasons why.

Joyful Copy Alignment: Answering why in your copy is one of the most important things you can do. It is another way to get in front of and overcome potential objections your customers may have to buying a product or service.

Lean into the Father and ask Him to show you which "reasons why" you should answer. I promise He will show you. Ecclesiastes 3 promises there is a reason for everything under heaven.

- (#) Reasons to (_____)
- Why (_____) Requires (_____)
- (#) Reasons Why You're Not (_____) (and What to Do about It)
- Why (_____) Improves Your (_____)
- Why (Surprising Fact)

Bold Promises Headline Framework

Create expectations by telling your reader what to expect. Share the WIIFM (What's in It For Me).

Joyful Copy Alignment: Only make promises you can fulfill and then follow through. Remember: Let your "yes" mean "yes" and "no" mean "no."

- The Ultimate Guide to (_____)
- The (#) Steps to (_____)
- The Only (_____) You'll Ever Need
- Everything You Need to Know about (_____) Being an Ethical Entrepreneur

- The Best Way to (_____) Write Joyful Headlines
- Make More (_____) with Your (_____)

How to Find Other Headline Examples

Headline frameworks are everywhere you look. One easy place to start is Google. Simply type in "headline frameworks," and as of this writing, you'll see more than thirteen million examples in less than a minute.

You'll find more examples that you might use when searching through Amazon, magazines, articles, and ads. The key is to look at what others have done and then determine how a similar approach might work best for you.

Remember, you are not looking at blueprints. You are looking at frameworks and examples that you will use to help write your own original content. Just be very careful that you don't copy a headline word for word, and make sure you're writing joyful copy without hype or manipulation. Ask the Lord to guide you, so you can apply it to YOUR business the way He wants you to.

You may wonder why I keep stressing some points over and over again. As humans, we require several reminders before an idea or concept sticks. So, I try to practice that old sales adage that I shared with you earlier: "Tell them what you're going to tell them. Tell them. Then tell them what you've told them." I know this process works, which is why I use it.

30

DO THIS NOW

You've written headlines to draw in readers, break up copy, and draw the eye. But how do you move people to the next step? How do you get people to take action?

The answer is easier than you think. You need to tell people what to do. It is that simple.

Since many people have difficulty making decisions, your copy will be stronger if you tell them what action to take.

Think about the last time you went out with friends or on a date with your husband. How did you like the "I dunno, where do you want to go" game? After the cuteness wore off, you probably found it frustrating because you just wanted a decision to be made. Right?! The same happens in marketing copy.

Help your prospective customer move to the next step by eliminating weighing the options. Make the next step clear and lead the way down the path you want them to take by telling them what to do next.

Remember the people who didn't attend a church service because no one asked? You need to avoid that with your audience by inviting them to take the next step.

James 4:2 says we don't have what we want because we don't ask God and don't get what we asked for because we ask with wrong motives. While that verse talks about asking God to act, you can also apply it to asking customers to act.

Translation: Ask customers to take the next steps, but do so with good intentions that do not involve twisting reality, hype, or manipulation.

Call To Action Exercise

[ACTION STEP] (Tab this section so you can refer to the Call to Action (CTA) tips and frameworks easily. Add the CTAs you create to your Reservoir of Information.)

HERE'S WHAT TO DO: As you continue building out your Reservoir of Information, you'll want to create a bank of Calls to Action (CTAs) to pull and use in your copy in the future. You'll always find opportunities to pepper CTAs on your web pages, sales pages, lead magnets, social posts, and even in your emails and blog posts.

You want to ensure that your CTAs are clear, concise requests that motivate people to take action. When you write good CTAs, they will convey value, create urgency (when needed), and give specific directions. The best CTAs are brief and use strong verbs:

- Access Now
- Act Now
- Book Your Adventure Now
- Book Your Free Call
- Discuss Your Options
- Download Now
- Free Trial
- Get Your Free Copy
- Join Now
- Learn More

- Register Now
- Subscribe Now

You will often see CTAs on clickable buttons or hyperlinks, but they can be in sentence form, too. Just remember that the shorter ones work best.

Here are some sentence examples:

- Mail your acceptance to me today.
- Act right now. You have nothing to lose and everything to gain.

Now that you understand why CTAs are needed and what they look like, take a moment to write some that you will use. For every Call to Action you write, ask yourself:

- What is your goal?
- What do you want your customer to do?

Just like all the exercises we've walked through before, ask Holy Spirit to help you determine what calls to action you need to create. Then write out as many variations as you can think of and add them to your Reservoir of Information.

31

FILTER YOUR
COPY FRAMEWORKS

O nce you've written headlines for the copy project you're working on, you'll want to review what you've written and filter it through at least three frameworks. I'm recommending these because I use them when I write copy.

Filter what you've written through the Four Us, AIDA, and *Joyful Copy* frameworks to make sure you align your copy and position it to work well.

NOTE: Since marketing involves testing, you may find that you need to tweak and revise your copy to see what works best with your audience. Marketing is never a one-and-done process. It is a continual journey where you will always find ways to improve.

Copy Filter Frameworks

[ACTION STEP] (Tab this section so you can refer to the headline tips and frameworks easily. You may want to just drop these three frameworks into your Reservoir of Information to keep everything in one place.)

Master Copywriter Michael Masterson is credited for creating the "Four U's Formula," and it is well-known and well-used by copywriters. It works extremely well in helping you ensure that what you've written will stand out and connect with your audience.

Four U's Framework

- **Useful** – Convey the benefit of reading what you've written.
- **Unique** – Share why what you've written is different.
- **Urgent** – Find ways to give a timeframe, e.g., now, today, or the first five (Note: You may not use this step every time.)
- **Ultra-Specific** – The more specific your copy is, the more useful and compelling it will be to your reader.

You should use urgency, which is definitely a component for writing good headlines, carefully and honestly. For example, if you say "The first five people…" OR "Sale ends in 24 hours," you must stick to what you've written. Not following through is manipulative and deceptive.

AIDA Framework

Advertising Hall of Famer Elias St. Elmo created the AIDA framework in 1898. It worked well then and still works today. This framework is well-used by copywriters even now.

AIDA, developed by St. Elmo Lewis in 1998, is an acronym for:

- Attention
- Interest
- Desire
- Action

To write any copy, including headlines, subheads, and bullets that attract and engage your audience, you need to know your audience well to speak their language when addressing their pain or problem.

When you write headlines for your content, ask yourself if what you've written:

- Captures your reader's **attention.**
- Addresses or educates about a specific point of **interest.**
- Offers a benefit they (already) **desire.**
- Inspires clear **action** by telling them what to do.

Joyful Copy Alignment Framework

We covered this concept throughout the book in several ways, but it bears repeating to make sure we are on the same page. Take one more step to make sure your words align with the fruits of the Spirit and characteristics of a Christ-follower. WHY? Because now more than ever, we see a hunger and need for Christ-following entrepreneurs to shine God's light and love in the world. Since God calls us to be set apart and not look like the world, our copy should look different, too.

While you may learn great marketing and writing concepts from other entrepreneurs and teachers, it is essential to run everything you use through God's Word to check for alignment. Galatians 5:14 teaches us that we are to demonstrate love for each other in everything we write and say.

If you see any marketing technique or writing framework that doesn't align with biblical principles, consider it a danger sign. Embrace the opportunity to take a stand, be different, and shine God's light in today's dark world. Make sure every word written or spoken about your business is *Joyful Copy*.

The way we position our products and services in the marketplace should exemplify love, joy, peace, patience, kindness, goodness, faithfulness, gentleness, and self-control (Galatians 5:22–23).

Since Philippians 4:8 teaches that Christ-followers should focus our thoughts on what is true, right, pure, honorable, lovely, and of good repute, our copy should likewise focus on the same attributes.

In contrast, our words should never use manipulation, hyper, or fear. In 1 Corinthians 10:24 the Bible says no one should seek their own good or interests, but the good and interests of others.

Two Easy Steps for *Joyful Copy* Alignment

ONE: Review what you've written to see if your copy is joyfully aligned or hints at twisted reality.

TWO: If you find words, phrases, or paragraphs that aren't **joyful**, rewrite that section to ensure alignment with the teachings of the Bible.

Refer to the *Joyful Copy* Checklist included with this book or access the latest version of it here: **https://www.joycapps.com/joyful-copy-alignment**

PART VI
REFLECTION QUESTIONS

Before you move into the last section, which contains many additional frameworks for pulling together your writing, let me encourage you to pause and reflect on your answers to these questions. Journaling your responses will help you see your growth and progress over time and remember clearly what Abba Father shares with you.

Points to Ponder

What do you focus on the most when you write or talk about your business? Yourself? Your products and services? Or the needs of your prospective customers?

Challenge: Determine where Holy Spirit wants you to shift your focus. Make a plan with Abba Father to get it done.

When you start each day, who do you focus on first?

Challenge: Before you do anything else at the beginning of every day and every project, be intentional to spend time talking to God and inviting Him in to partner with you. Read His Word and apply it to every aspect of your life and business.

What have you been putting off that requires you to act? Write it down.

Challenge: Ask God to help you navigate the list. Don't be surprised if He has you eliminate a few items and add something you hadn't previously considered.

PART VII: DELIVER
JOYFUL COPY

32

DELIVER: PULLING IT ALL TO-
GETHER (CLOSING REMARKS)

If you've read through all the chapters, worked through the exercises, and answered the reflection questions, you are well on your way to writing joyful copy. Congratulations!

This final section will give you a few frameworks for pulling together copy you can use in a variety of ways. I'm closing out the book with a handful of framework options to get you started pulling together everything from the previous chapters.

Before you jump in, I need to reiterate that every piece you create should be guided by Holy Spirit. Ask Him to help you use the insights you've gleaned from His Word and this book to create a strategy for connecting with your customers. Pray about it. Ask Him specific questions. Then take action on what He says to do.

I also strongly recommend that you invest the time to put together a communications strategy before diving headlong into writing copy for web pages or sales pages. Ask God to help you determine your objective, goals, and tactics you'll need to see results.

Strategy is vital to any Christ-following entrepreneur who needs to deliver to the world what God has called you to do. While this book addresses how to use words to connect with customers by showing up ethically and authentically, it does not address putting together a communications strategy. (While it is a service I offer, perhaps that is another book, course, or talk I'll offer in the future. For now, Shae Bynes has an excellent book called *The Kingdom Driven Entrepreneur's Guide to Goal Setting* that I highly recommend as a starting point.)

When you know Abba's objective and goals for your business, you'll see how beautifully joyful copy fits into your messaging, web pages, and sales page frameworks for connecting with your customers.

The following frameworks are not a one-size-fits-all approach. I'm offering these to help you get started. The best framework for laying out joyful copy will come out of your partnership with Holy Spirit and working with other Christ-following entrepreneurs skilled in marketing strategy and copywriting. Even if you don't write the copy yourself, knowing the process that goes into it will help you manage your business and connect with your customers in many ways.

To deliver solid messaging, you need to outline the key messages about your business and offering. (I've provided a messaging framework to help you below my closing signature.) To do that, I suggest going back through the notes and exercises you saved in your Reservoir of Information and using them to outline your messaging.

Once you outline your messaging framework, use those key points in your web pages, social posts, sales pages, emails, product descriptions, etc. Since examples for writing content for each of those items could result in multiple standalone books and courses, I'm giving you one website copy framework and a few sales page examples to whet your appetite. As you thumb through the next few pages, you will find:

1. Your Messaging Framework
2. What to Do Before You Write*
3. Website Copy Framework
4. Sales Page Framework (Option 1)
5. Sales Page Framework (Option 2)
6. Sales Page (Example 1)
7. Sales Page (Example 2)
8. What to Do After You Write*

*We addressed some of these items earlier. Since it is vitally important that you incorporate these concepts into your writing prep, I included them in the frameworks again.

I also hope you'll check out the How-to Guide Power Tools and Key Principles for each chapter in the Appendix, located after the frameworks.

Thank you for taking the time to read through Joyful Copy. If you have any questions, feel free to reach out to me directly at Joy@JoyCapps.com.

Until our paths cross again, my God richly bless you for partnering with Him in all you think, say, do, and may all your copy be Joyful.

Philippians 1:3–6,

Joy

Your Messaging Framework

Before you write, you need to start with the end in mind. Working through Your Messaging Framework will help you prepare for what you write in the future. Follow the steps one by one to create your outline.

How to Organize

- Use this template to outline your messaging by pulling key points from your Reservoir of Information (the notes you took as you worked through each chapter).

- Put all of the following in a Google sheet or Excel spreadsheet or on a Google doc or Word doc.

- Save it so you can refer back to it often.

Your Messaging Framework (8 steps)

- Reviewing your Reservoir of Information, select your best Messaging Framework and pick the best one to use.
- List the issues/problems your customers experience outwardly and internally.
  - Outside factors (common problems)
  - Inside factors (common fears and motivations)
- Write out the top emotions they feel about these external and internal issues.
- List what you understand about their specific problems, fears, emotions, and motivators.
  - Write 1-3 ways you empathize with each. Make sure what you write is authentic and not made up.
  - Examples:
    - "We understand how it feels to...," "Nobody should have to experience...," "Like you, we're frustrated by..."
    - Show what you have in common with them: "I know how you feel because..."
    - Use their language and words that show you see, hear, and understand them.
- Showcase your expertise and authority.
  - Write at least three 1-2 sentence testimonials.
  - Pull together statistics about results others have experienced
  - List any relevant awards or certifications
  - Collect any logos from customers you've worked with
- Offers:
  - What products/services do you offer?
  - What are the top 3-5 benefits of each?

- Action:
  o What do you want them to do?
  o Pull out specific calls to actions you'll use.
- Results:
  o What success will they experience by working with you or your solution?
  o How will what you offer help them solve their problem?

Once you have completed this outline, use it to help you create content for connecting with your audience. I encourage you to reference back to the points in Your Messaging Framework for the various types of communications and marketing content you write.

What to Do Before You Write

Did you know that good writing begins with planning? Just like planning a vacation, you'll experience better results when you map the route before taking off for your destination. If you start with the end in mind, you'll make stronger connections with your audience. All you need to do is answer the following questions BEFORE you write. Try it. I promise you'll see results.

- Who is your audience for this piece of copy you're writing?
- What is the goal of what you're writing?
- Are there links you need to include?
- What specific Calls to Action do you need to include?
- What do you want the reader to do? (Tell them.)
- Is there ONE thread or storyline you could use to make your point?

- What are the key points of that ONE thread? (Try to use three points or fewer.)

- What pain point(s) are you addressing for your customer in this copy?

- Is what you're writing interesting to your audience or only to you? (If only to you, revise. Focus on THEM.)

- Do you have a one- or two-sentence pull quote or testimonial to validate what you're saying?

Website Copy Framework

The following framework provides an outline for copy for specific website pages. This example shows the copy portion only for a few key pages, e.g., Home, Services/Courses, About Pages. While you may need or want frameworks that include other types of pages, they will typically follow similar frameworks and always pull from your Reservoir of Information.

As you look at the framework, you will notice screenshots from several different types of websites to provide an example. I used a variety to give you ideas on what your copy might look like after you've written it or had someone write it for you. While it would seem logical to include links to every business I included, I know that websites change over time and sometimes servers go down. With that in mind, I've included screenshots from a specific point in time with permission from each client.

- Before you begin, map out the primary pages needed for your site. I suggest keeping your top-level navigation down to three or four pages.

- While you will always have a home page, determine if your business needs a page for Services, Courses, Blog, About,

Coaching, Workshops, Resources, Events, Media, Speaking, etc.

- Use your Messaging Outline and Reservoir of Information to help you build out the content for your pages.

- Save what you're working on periodically to avoid losing any work.

- Realize that you will write and edit several versions along the way.

Home Page

Insert your URL here. (Example: www.yourwebsitename.com/)

Try not to write HOME in your top-level nav. Instead make your logo clickable and make it lead back to your home page.

Home | **Services / Courses** | **About**

Overview: Everything should be brief and scannable. (Copy dense is a no-go.) Writing one- or two-sentence paragraphs with occasional bulleted lists and bolding words to draw the eye makes it easier to read.

While *every* website is different, *every* home page should clearly tell visitors the problem you solve, specifically who you solve it for, and how you solve it. Consider using this framework from top to bottom of your page with five "sections" of copy that you'll balance with photos and graphic images. Here's an overview of what is in each section.

Section 1: Your God-Given Message Framework with a specific Call to Action

Section 2: Focus on Customer Issues

- Ask questions about their issues to connect with them.
- Show your understanding of their problems. (See survey results.)

Section 3: Show your authority. (Give stats about results, certifications, or logos.)

Section 4: What others say. Include a slider with two or three 1-2 sentence quotes (testimonials).

Section 5: Show the success and transformation your clients will experience.

Pepper Calls to Action throughout the sections in a well-balanced manner.

Section 1 Home Page Examples

Below are several examples of Home Page *Section One* copy. Since websites continually change, it is easier to show you screenshots than give you URLs to websites that might have changed.

Example 1: Agility Coaching

Example 2: Marriage and Business Coach for Entrepreneurs and Couples (Faith-Based)

Example 3: Coaching for Families and Individuals (Faith-Based)

Example 4: Scents for Deer Hunters

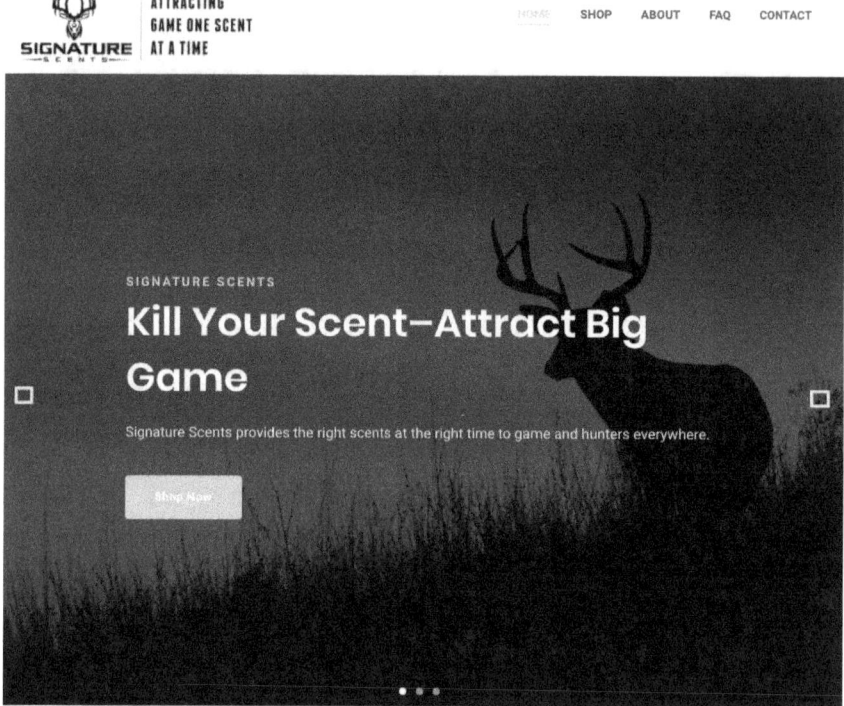

Example 5: Copywriting and Business Coach (This is a previous version of my website's section one.)

Example 6: Insurance Wholesaler targeting Insurance Agents and Brokers

(Note: This home page uses a slider that rotates through a series of images with multiple messages and call to actions. (You see the white dots below the CTA button? Each dot represents a slider with a different message. I'm only sharing one message with you here.)

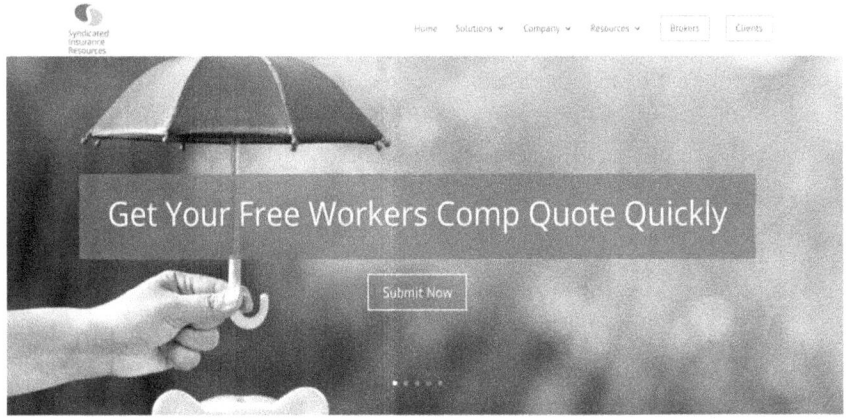

Syndicated Insurance Resources: Strategic Risk
Management Solutions for Business

Now, let's look at the section one framework for your home page.

Section 1: God-Given Message Framework with Call to Action

HERE'S WHAT TO DO:

- Pull from previous exercises to write out who you help, what problem you solve, and how you solve it.

- Tell them what to do by giving a call to action (CTA).

- Learn More, Discuss Your Needs, Let's Talk, Let Us Help You, Download (XYZ-thing of value), etc.

- For future planning, you'll want to think about and map out what happens when someone clicks that call-to-action button.

- Where will your first section CTA button take people?

  o To a pop-up form? To another page on your website?

- If the call-to-action button leads to a form, what happens when they complete it?

  o Do they receive a confirmation or thank you email?

  o Do they receive a download?

  o Will they receive a series of emails telling them how to use the download?

- If the button leads to another page, what helpful instruction will they find there?

Section 2 Home Page Examples

As you look at the different *Section Two* examples below, notice how they ask and answer a specific question. You will want to do the same to draw your customers in. Remember: Asking questions creates connections.

Example 3: Coaching for Entrepreneurs and Couples (Faith-Based)

Ready to end the power struggle between your business & marriage?

Power Couples by Design™ will help you resolve:

· Financial stress
· Poor communication issues
· Inconsistent profitability
· Work-life-play balance
· And much more

Let's Talk.

Example 2: Coaching for Families and Individuals (Faith-Based)

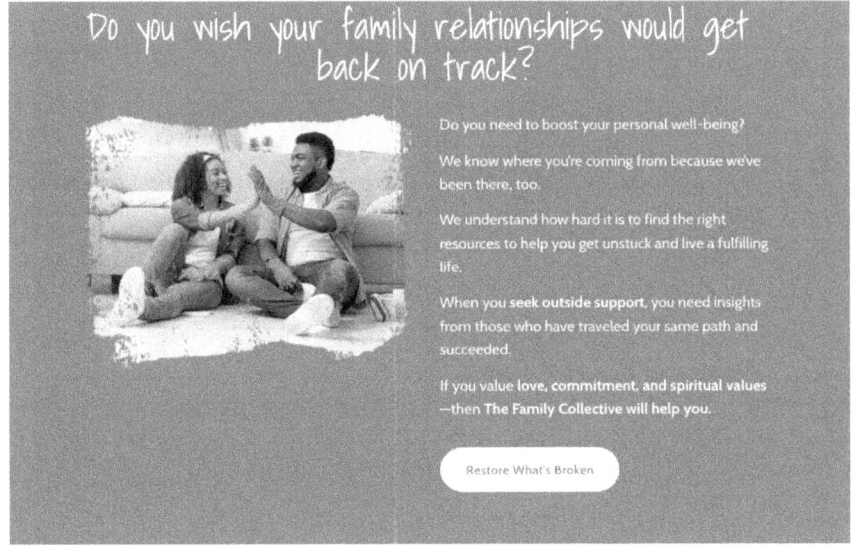

Example 3: Copywriting and Business Coach (This is a previous version of my website's section two.)

Now, let's look at the Section 2 framework for your home page.

Section 2: Focus on the Issues/Opportunities They Want/Need That You Solve

HERE'S WHAT TO DO:

1. Ask a specific question about their issue. (Use your headline frameworks and information from your surveys and Reservoir of Information.)

2. Show your understanding of their problems. (Refer to Outline Your Messaging document, your survey findings, and your Reservoir of Information.)

3. Show you know how they feel. Consider weaving in your personal experience to show you understand. (Weave in their top emotions.)

You can use two or three buttons for customers to self-identify what they want, which will lead them to your product/services that address specific needs. For example, you may place what you offer, e.g., coaching, events, and copywriting each on a separate clickable button that leads to a full sales page for that service or product.

Section 3 Home Page Examples

Some home pages may not have a section showcasing expertise and authority. If your home page does, you can easily highlight your success using logos. This area offers a variety of ways to show logos of people and companies you've worked with or where you've received publicity.

Below are a few examples of what that might look like. Of course, you'll want to use logos and awards that represent you and your business.

Example 1:

Example 2:

As Seen On...

Example 3:

Example 4:

We've Helped...

Example 5:

Note: This highly customized example is different because the Deer Scent company wanted to focus on how they give back to the environment, which is a key differentiator that is important to their target audience.

Example 6: Insurance Wholesaler targeting Insurance Agents and Brokers

Note: This highly customized example is different because the Insurance Wholesaler wanted to show their target audience (Insurance Brokers and Agents) how they help find insurance quotes that provide cost savings. In this example, they highlighted a rotating series showing the dollar amount of insurance policies they bound. (Binding is another way to say contract using insurance language.)

Section 3: Show Your Expertise and Authority

HERE'S WHAT TO DO:

- Consider including a logo bar with former client logos, awards, or certifications you possess.

- Instead of a logo bar, you may include a section or rotating banner of stats/results from working with you.

- Peppering statistics throughout the copy on your pages is another option, too.

Section Four Home Page Examples

Some people have one page dedicated to testimonials, but I've observed that testimonials are more powerful when spread throughout your website. It is a bonus if you can use the first and last name with a picture and business name. But if you cannot, show what you can comfortably show as long as it is truthful and not fabricated. Consider these examples below.

Example 1: Coaching for Families and Individuals (Faith-Based) Testimonial with Anonymity

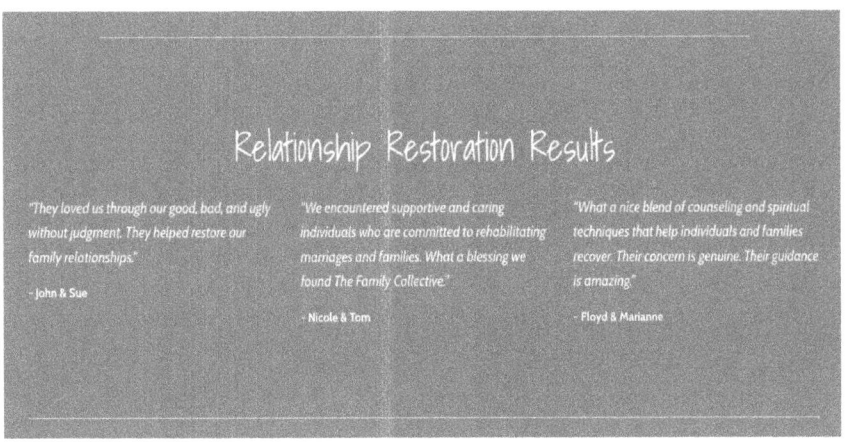

Relationship Restoration Results

"They loved us through our good, bad, and ugly without judgment. They helped restore our family relationships."
— John & Sue

"We encountered supportive and caring individuals who are committed to rehabilitating marriages and families. What a blessing we found The Family Collective."
— Nicole & Tom

"What a nice blend of counseling and spiritual techniques that help individuals and families recover. Their concern is genuine. Their guidance is amazing."
— Floyd & Marianne

Example 2: Coaching for Entrepreneurs and Couples (Faith-Based) Testimonial

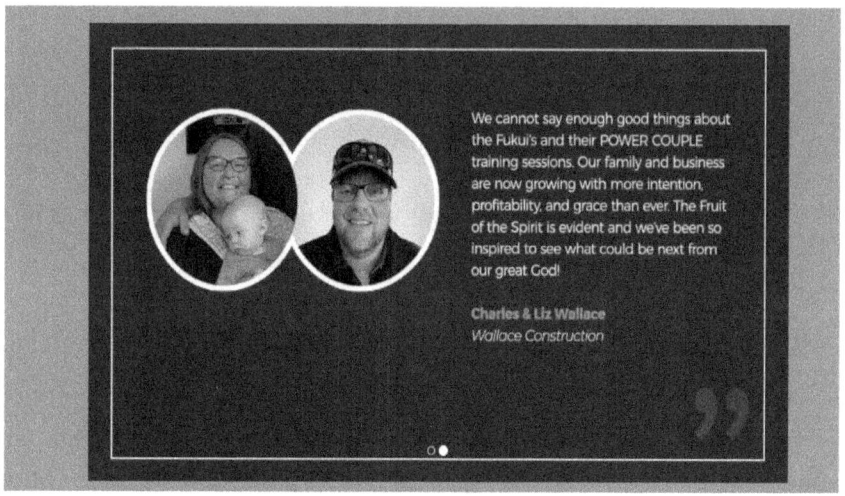

We cannot say enough good things about the Fukui's and their POWER COUPLE training sessions. Our family and business are now growing with more intention, profitability, and grace than ever. The Fruit of the Spirit is evident and we've been so inspired to see what could be next from our great God!

Charles & Liz Wallace
Wallace Construction

Example 3: Agility Coach Testimonials with Anonymity

What Our Satisfied Clients Are Saying...

Greater Confidence and Visibility	**People Noticed the Transformation**	**My Mindset Changed and Business Grew**	**Sales Results Increased by 600%**
"With my thoughts and actions aligned, I improved my communication style. My **performance & personal brand become stronger,** and soon after working with Chuen Chuen, I took on a **new leadership role.**"	Chuen Chuen coached me to tap into my strengths. **My motivation increased,** which helped me become very proactive at my workplace. I began showing up differently - more authenticity and ease.	My mindset has changed from a freelancer to a business owner. With effective leadership skills, I became **actively engaged in growing my company** and responding to **new opportunities** with agility.	"My sales results improved by 600% **in just 3 sessions.** Reevaluating **my strengths helped** me leverage them effectively. I can now **shine as a leader and be more than a manager.**"
Suguna, Education Management Professional	Chun, Veteran Finance Professional	Wei, Entrepreneur	Eileen T., Sales Director, Financial Services

Example 4: Massage Therapist Testimonials with Anonymity

What People Say About Amy...

"Amy is knowledgeable and professional and when I left I felt 100% better. I highly recommend her to anyone needing a great massage at a great price."

— Michael D.

"Not going to lie, I was skeptical at first. But I really like Amy's haircare products. My hair is super soft. It feels clean and I don't have to wash it every day now."

— Ellie K.

"I have been to several places and can say this is the best one! Thanks Amy! A must go to for your next massage."

— Susan K.

Example 5: Copywriting and Business Coach Testimonial (from my website)

"Writing compelling marketing and sales copy is a core discipline for every business owner to learn, but getting training on how to write in an authentic way that is aligned with your values is essential. Joy Capps is a resource you can trust to help you do just that!"

Shae Bynes

Example 6: Insurance Wholesaler targeting Insurance Agents and Brokers

Syndicated Insurance Resources has a more holistic, hands-on approach. They always know the best vendor for the need and have very creative solutions for those difficult to place risks. Using their tools and resources shaves time off, which allows me to be more productive and successful.

Mark McGhee
Momentum Capital Holdings, LLC

Section 4: Include Two or Three Testimonials (aka Pull Quotes)

HERE'S WHAT TO DO:

- Pull testimonials from your Reservoir of Information
- Keep the quotes you use short and sweet.
- Use only one or two sentences per person.
- Include a name, logo, headshot, and position whenever possible.
- Unless required for anonymity, avoid using a first name and last initial only because it appears to be a fabrication.
- Ensure what others say about you is believable and relatable.

Services Page

Insert your URL here.

Example: www.yourwebsitename.com/services (<—The page name will reflect what you call this page. If you call it services, it will read services. If you call it coaching, it will read coaching, and so on.)

Home | **Services / Courses** | About

<u>Overview:</u> Your services page may be labeled "Coaching" and talk about your coaching services. Or it may just say "Copywriting" and dive into that topic. If you sell hair care products or deer scents, your services page may use a simple one-word descriptor and focus on that product or service. "Services" has a variety of meanings in different business models.

As always, everything you write should be brief and scannable. Remember, being copy dense is a no-go. Writing one- to two-sentence paragraphs with occasional bulleted lists and bolding words to draw the eye makes the material easier to read.

Services / Courses Page Examples

Example 1: Hair product page – Section 1

Example 1: Hair product page – Section 2

Are you searching for customized haircare solutions that fix:

- color or heat damage
- dryness
- dullness
- frizziness
- split ends
- oily scalp

Look no further. Find the right hair solutions to create hair happiness.

Take FREE Hair Quiz Now.

Example 2: Coaching for Entrepreneurs and Couples – Coaching Page – Section 1

Example 2: Coaching for Entrepreneurs and Couples – Coaching Page – Section 2

Example 2: Coaching for Entrepreneurs and Couples – Coaching Page – Section 3

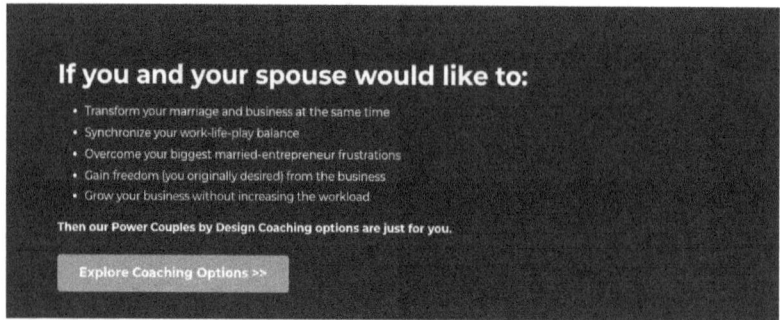

Example 3: Copywriting Services – Section 1

Sell Your Products & Services Using Trustworthy Copy.

Let Me Help You.

Example 3: Copywriting Services – Section 2

Are Your Words Connecting & Converting?

As a business leader, you're eager to reach customers who need the transformation you offer.

You know the right words will help you connect, sell, persuade, influence, inform, promote, and position your solutions.

There's only one problem. Writing isn't your forte. In fact, writing is your least favorite thing to do.

Explore Copywriting Options

Example 3: Copywriting Services – Section 3

Acknowledge Your Pain.

While others find writing easy or even (gasp!) fun, you'd rather watch paint dry instead of writing.

You know a 100 better ways to spend your time instead of putting words together to that connect, evoke emotion, and deliver value.

You need compelling copy to reach your business goals and convey your message to the world ethically.

Discuss Writing Support

Example 3: Copywriting Services – Section 4 (at the bottom of my copywriting services page)

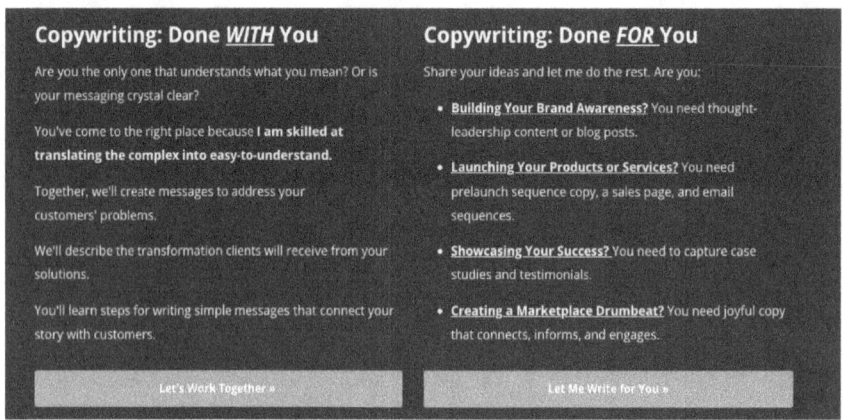

Example 4: Group Coaching for Families and Individuals – Section 1

Example 4: Group Coaching for Families and Individuals – Section 2

Share Common Hurdles. Go Deeper in Your Relationships.

Let's face it, navigating obstacles and challenges by yourself is hard.

Shared community helps you make progress faster, especially when you're with like-minded individuals and couples.

The Family Collective offers **three groups** that **meet in 8-week sessions** throughout the year.

With **new group** sessions starting **throughout the year,** there are many options from which to choose.

Learn more and sign up for group sessions about:

MARRIAGE FOR COUPLES · SEXUAL PURITY FOR MEN · IDENTITY FOR WOMEN

Example 4: Group Coaching for Families and Individuals – Section 3

Transform Your Marriage? Yes, Please.

- Are you satisfied with your marriage?
- Is the silent treatment getting old?
- Want to spice up your love life?
- Tired of not being heard?

No matter how long you've been married, there's always room for improvement.

Good News! **Real intimacy, lasting connection, and authentic communication are possible.**

Get more out of your relationship when you **join our LIVE 8-week Marriage Group for only $39 per couple + $9.99 for the workbook.**

Offered three times a year, this interactive group will work through our workbook *Face-to-Face: Growing Connection, Cultivating Intimacy.*

Learn More & Register Now.

Example 4: Group Coaching for Families and Individuals – Section 4 (at the bottom of the FAQs page)

YOU'VE GOT QUESTIONS.

WE'VE GOT ANSWERS.

• ARE THE GROUPS CONFIDENTIAL?

• DO GROUPS MEET IN PERSON OR ONLINE?

• WHY IS THERE A CHARGE FOR GROUP SESSIONS?

• WILL YOU BE ADDING MORE GROUPS?

• HOW DO I SHARE AN IDEA FOR A GROUP OR GET CONSIDERED FOR LEADING A GROUP?

Example 5: Insurance Wholesaler targeting Insurance Agents and Brokers – Section 1

Note: With multiple product lines, this example was customized to showcase all their offerings with clickable links that led to other dedicated product pages.

SOLUTIONS

Syndicated Insurance Resources provides insurance brokers with solutions to help employers.

Stop spending hours researching the various offerings your customer need. We've done the hard work for you by bringing everything together in one online dashboard. Our collaborative process saves you time and money.

With the click of a button, your obligation-free registration gives you access to an array product options and markets only available through our innovative technology and partnerships.

We offer alternative risk management, pay-as-you-go administration and HR consulting services that are guaranteed to set you apart from your competitors. By working with us, you receive competitive commissions that are paid quickly and regularly, too.

Grow Your Book of Business	Access Alternative Risk Solutions	Increase Workers Comp Options	Provide HR Consulting Services	Earn Competitive Commissions

Example 5: Insurance Wholesaler targeting Insurance Agents and Brokers – Section 2

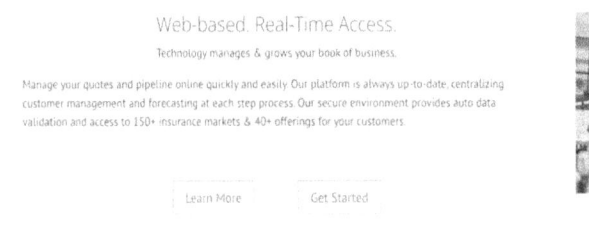

Web-based. Real-Time Access.

Technology manages & grows your book of business.

Manage your quotes and pipeline online quickly and easily. Our platform is always up-to-date, centralizing customer management and forecasting at each step process. Our secure environment provides auto data validation and access to 150+ insurance markets & 40+ offerings for your customers.

Learn More   Get Started

Example 5: Insurance Wholesaler targeting Insurance Agents and Brokers – Section 3

Lower Costs. Reduce Overhead.

Provide Total Employer Support

Increase retention rates with centralized contractor management with our staffing and PEO options. Stay involved with the account. Maintain your relationship and commission income. Use one or many of our alternative market solutions to increase your client's workload flexibility.

Show Me How   Get Started

Example 5: Insurance Wholesaler targeting Insurance Agents and Brokers – Section 4

Save Time. Increase Market Access.

Get WC Quotes Faster.

Connect with A-rated carriers for quick, accurate online quotes with competitive pricing and great commissions. Leverage our single-point-of-contact and Appulate partnership to access nearly 200 market combinations. Tap into our national network of resources to get fast WC certificates and pay-as-you-go.

Learn More   Get Started

Example 5: Insurance Wholesaler targeting Insurance Agents and Brokers – Section 5

Stand Out from Competitors. Offer More Benefits.

Provide HR Consulting Services to Your Customers.

Use our national network of professionals to provide HR Consulting services to your employer customers Proactively give your customers control over risks while saving money. From Legal & Labor Law to Compliance Training, our experts provide immediate answers and resolve business issues.

Offer More   Get Started

Example 5: Insurance Wholesaler targeting Insurance Agents and Brokers – Section 6

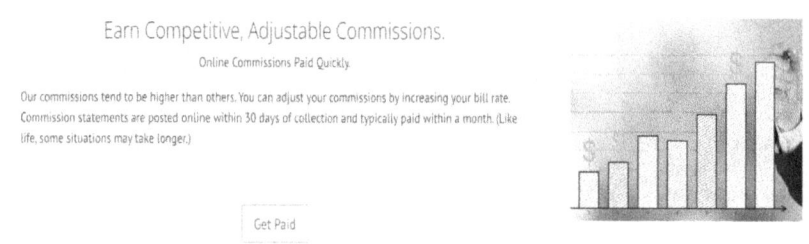

Earn Competitive, Adjustable Commissions.

Online Commissions Paid Quickly.

Our commissions tend to be higher than others. You can adjust your commissions by increasing your bill rate. Commission statements are posted online within 30 days of collection and typically paid within a month. (Like life, some situations may take longer.)

Get Paid

Your products/services page can look many different ways. You may want to provide a snippet about each solution with a call-to-action button that leads to a more robust dedicated page for that solution.

HERE'S WHAT TO DO:

Once you decide what you need for your services/course page, you always want to include:

- Questions that address your customers' problems and show that you know how they feel
- Benefits they will experience
- A short product description

- Reasons WHY your product or service will help them experience results
- Call-to-action buttons that tell them what to do
- Addressing any objections throughout your copy
- An FAQ as shown in the last example above
- A testimonial or success metric whenever possible

About Page

Insert your URL here.

Example: www.yourwebsitename.com/about

Home | Services/Courses | About

Overview: As always, everything should be brief and scannable. (Again, copy dense is a no-go.) Writing one- to two-sentence paragraphs with occasional bulleted lists and bolding words to draw the eye makes it easier to read.

In the interest of space in this book, I'm only including a couple of very different examples of the About Page. Please know that there are *many ways* to create an effective About Page that I share in my *Joyful Copy* 1-on-1 coaching, courses, and Done-For- and Done-With-You Services.

Example 1: Copywriting and Marketing – Done-For or With-You

Note: By the time this book goes to print, I will update my website again, but my example below will give you a good idea of *one* way to do it.

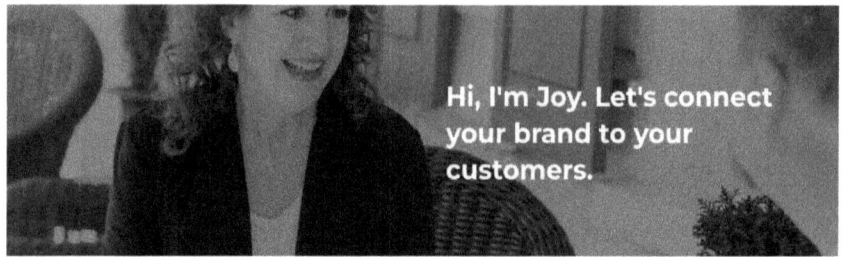

Hi, I'm Joy. Let's connect your brand to your customers.

Hi, and welcome!

If you're interested in reading my bio, story, or mission, you will find them further down this page.

But first let's chat about how I help entrepreneurs just like you.

With a **heart to serve others**, I've been **writing copy and creating values-based strategy for business owners** for more than 20 years.

It may sound geeky, but I genuinely enjoy translating entrepreneurial visions into customized roadmaps, engaging content, and words that connect with customers.

As a life-long student, I continue to study the masters and apply best practices FOR and WITH my clients. The techniques I use come from studying others like Gary Halbert, James Wedmore, Jeff Walker, John Carlton, Mike Kim, Ray Edwards, and many others.

But my biggest writing influence comes from the principles in God's Word. (Yes, you read that correctly. Biblical principles have a LOT to say about writing authentically and clearly.)

Are you an entrepreneurial business owner who:

- **Desires joyful copy that energizes and connects with your ideal customers?**
- **Needs to build your brand, launch products, or engage your list?**
- **Wants to share how your offerings solve the problems that keep your customers up at night?**

Everything starts with a conversation, so let's talk about your needs.

If we're not the right fit, I'll try to point you to someone else to help you reach your goals.

Click the button for an initial conversation now.

Thank you for your interest. I welcome the opportunity to help you reach your audience authentically.

Committed to Serving Others,

Joy

Prov. 16:3 & 9

Schedule Your Discovery Call Now.

When I'm in my happy place, you'll find me playing "underwater tourist" scuba diving looking for photo opportunities as I explore God's creations.

When I'm on land, I help business owners use joyful copywriting and values-based business coaching to connect their brand with customers.

Over the past 20+ years, I have worked with many small businesses, startups, and personal brands. Some have gone public, while others have quietly done well in their niche.

I've also supported notable brands such as Marvel Comics Creator Stan Lee, Compaq Computer Corp., and Enron. Along my journey, I've also worked for thought leaders like The John Maxwell Team, Michael Hyatt & Co., Ray Edwards, and Mike Kim and niche brands you may never encounter.

As a seasoned expert, I do not profess to know it all. But I possess a good deal of practical know-how, seasoned experience, and wisdom-based insights.

Rest assured, I deliver on my promises and strive to exceed my clients' expectations.

Learn More About Me

My Story

My Mission

Let's use joyful copywriting and values-based business coaching to connect with your customers.

Let's Get Started! »

Example 2: Insurance Wholesaler targeting Insurance Agents and Brokers

Note: As a company, they wanted a way to share about their company and how they help their customers. This page reflects what the insurance wholesaler desired.

About Us.

Syndicated Insurance Resources help brokers competitively increase their employer-focused insurance programs and HR management offerings. Our leading technology automation, strategic industry partnerships and comprehensive professional services provide high commissions while growing a broker's book of business. With access to more than 150 markets and 40+ program offerings, we provide a broker marketplace for competitive insurance offerings.

A free Syndicated Services account provides insurance brokers with a dashboard of options that provide save time and money. Access our broker portal for:

- Quick policy quotes from a wide array of markets
- Instant access to Appulate ACORD data management portal
- Robust technology to manage and grow your book of business
- Bundled or à la carte staffing options
- Unrestricted payment options using the payroll provider of your client's choice
- Various HR consulting services to beef up your competitive offerings

Streamline Your Business

Why Syndicated Insurance Resources?

We provide unprecedented A-rated market access and programs. Combined with cutting-edge technology and exceptional customer service, we partner with brokers and companies to make them champions. Since 1995, we've worked hard to become a trusted resource for brokers.

We partner with you to grow your book of business and raise your commissions. Our expertise and access creates a win-win environment for you.

Get Started

Our Leadership Team.

Working together for more than 30 years, our core team has built (and sold) billion dollar companies that specialize in human resources, workers compensation and employee benefits outsourcing. Our diverse group brings unparalleled experience dedicated to meet the needs of insurance brokers.

Company Directory   Contact Us

Example 3: Coaching for Families and Individuals (Faith-Based)

Note: They wanted a way to share who they represent, the founders, and then several partners they recommend. In the screenshots below, I'm only including the first few panels without the recommended partners, due to the length of About their page.

Who is The Family Collective?

The Family Collective restores, rebuilds, and renews personal connections—one person at a time.

We help individuals and family members realize their unique potential by making healthy relationships a reality.

Our coaching programs meet people where they are in their pain and desire to improve.

Hi, We're Neal & Diane Arnold.

We are passionate about restoring individuals, families, and marriages by using lessons from our personal crises and professional know-how.

With more than 38 years of marriage, three sons, three daughter-in-laws, and a beautiful grand-daughter—we've overcome tragedies most never survive. Together, we're a poster couple for taking what the enemy meant for evil and using it for good.

Diane is a Licensed Professional Counselor with family and marriage counseling specialties. With an expertise in overcoming trauma and betrayal, she's a certified EFT and EMDR therapist. Her work is published and shows remarkable results.

As a successful executive in the financial industry, Neal is adept at helping souls prosper as they mend wounds and reach something greater.

We created The Family Collective to help everyone realize their fullest potential and transform lives around the world.

LEARN MORE

CONTACT US

EMAIL NEAL & DIANE

HERE'S WHAT TO DO:

Consider using this framework from top to bottom of your page:

- Section 1: Why you do what you do; CTA
- Section 2: Fun fact bio; drill deeper by highlighting key points from your background
- Section 3: Share your story in a short, relatable way.
- Section 4: Share your mission in a short, relatable way.

Pepper Calls to Action throughout the sections in a well-balanced manner. While there are many ways to write an About page, some of these examples should help you get started.

Sales Page Framework (Option 1)

Summary:

The goal is to write a sales page to sell the benefits of paying x amount to join, register, or buy XYZ.

Every sales page you write should follow frameworks that include but are not limited to writing clear, concise copy that:

- Is easy to scan.
- Hones in on your customers' problems.
- Focuses on what they want/need.
- Offers a solution to their problem.
- Shows results (using testimonials).
- Gives an offer.
- Tells what to do next.

Bolding keywords and phrases throughout is intentional. Using colors, spacing, graphic icons, etc., will help break up the copy while drawing the eye.

The headlines and subheads you use should:

- Draw the reader in because it speaks to them specifically.
- Allow the reader to scan and understand the call to action.

This example is written as one long-form sales page, and noted section breaks are for design purposes only.

To make this more robust, you could also include:

1. FAQs, but you would need to list and answer questions you typically receive.
2. Your clearly defined guarantee.
3. Additional objections you typically receive when selling this to others. (Remember you want to address objections in your copy before your prospective customer raises the question.)

HERO SECTION 1:

HEADER IMAGE: Logo top right overlay on a greyed-out image with the lead (aka eyebrow copy) at the top, which says precisely who the sales page is written to address. Here's an example of eyebrow copy.

ATTENTION: If you're an (xyz specific niche person), this (xyz solutions/offer/event/product) is for you...

(headline)

Clear Headline Honed In on Problem

(subhead)

Clear Subhead to support and expand on the problem while hinting at a solution

(Add bold CTA button on the bottom of the image OR right below the subhead)

Tell them what to do<——Clear CTA button copy

(Link the CTA button to jump to the place on the page where sign-up details or offers are listed.)

SECTION 2:

(paragraph copy)

Sub-headline to draw in the reader

Supporting copy that expands on that headline

(subhead)

Sub-headline to draw in the reader (emphasize wants/needs)

(paragraph copy)

Supporting copy that expands on the subhead for this section

- Bulleted list with you supporting point
- Bulleted list with you supporting point
- Bulleted list with you supporting point

Consider using a bulleted list and bolding keywords

SECTION 3:

(subhead)

Sub-headline to speak to the reader (show your understanding)

(paragraph copy)

Supporting copy that expands on the subhead for this section

- Bulleted list with you supporting point
- Bulleted list with you supporting point
- Bulleted list with you supporting point

Consider using a bulleted list and bolding keywords

Tell them what to do <——Clear CTA button copy

(Link the CTA button to jump to the place on the page where sign-up details or offers are listed.)

SECTION 4:

(subhead)

Sub-headline to draw in the reader (answer whys)

(paragraph copy)

Supporting copy that expands on the subhead for this section

- Bulleted list with you supporting point
- Bulleted list with you supporting point
- Bulleted list with you supporting point

Consider using a bulleted list and bolding keywords

SECTION 5:

(subhead)

Sub-headline to speak to the prospective customer

(offer your solution to their problem)

(paragraph copy)

Supporting copy that defines your solution clearly

SECTION 6:

Consider using a different background color by starting a new section to help text flow and draw the eye.

(paragraph copy continued)

If needed, more supporting copy that defines your solution clearly.

Tell them what to do <——Clear CTA button copy

(Link the CTA button to jump to the place on the page where sign-up details or offers are listed.)

SECTION 7:

(subhead)

Sub-headline setting up testimonials (e.g., what others have to say OR don't take my word for it…)

(testimonial copy)

SECTION 8:

(subhead)

Sub-headline asking if they are ready for xyz solution to their specific problem/need

(paragraph copy)

Supporting copy that clearly restates their problem and your solution

Tell them what to do <—Clear CTA button copy

(Link the CTA button to jump to the place on the page where sign-up details or offers are listed.)

SECTION 9:

Consider using a different background color by starting a new section to help text flow and draw the eye.

(paragraph copy continued)

If needed, additional supporting copy about your offer

SECTION 10:

Headline with your offer (focus on benefits, not features)

Light supporting copy with CLEAR CTA for responding to your offer

Tell them what to do <—Clear CTA button copy

(Link the CTA button to jump to the place on the page where sign-up details or offers are listed.)

SECTION: 11

(subhead)

Subhead to set up your FAQs

Questions and answers (clear and concise copy)

1)

2)

3)

Etc.

SECTION: 12

Restate your offer (focus on benefits, not features)

Light supporting copy with CLEAR CTA for responding to your offer

Large, bold, CTA button

Tell them what to do!

Sales Page Framework (Option 2)

Summary: The following sales page framework is generic in nature and should be modified to fit each product or service you are selling. This version is considered short by copywriting standards.

The goal is to elevate your prospects awareness of their problem by poking at it and agitating it. You ask your prospect to buy AFTER you offer the solution. Be sure to follow the "rule of one" throughout the copy:

- one customer you're trying to convert into a sale
- one big idea
- one promise
- one offer

Approach

PAS: problem, agitate, solve

AIDA: attention, interest, desire, action

Joyful Copy: aligns with the fruits of the Spirit

- **Remind your reader about their problem**

  o Emphasize that problem
  o Then solve it

- **Always speak to the emotions of one customer based on your research** – not what you think you know.

  o You will connect with your audience when you speak about what is on their heart and mind.

  o Use the voice of the customer with their actual words and phrases.

- **Make sure your <u>one big idea</u> includes**:

  o What your ideal customer wants badly
  o Stating your big idea in a unique way
  o Drawing your ideal customer in to learn more to see what's possible or start believing you

- **Write one promise that states the ultimate result/benefit from using your product/service**

Breakdown/Flow (8 Sections)

Section 1: Header

- Big benefit/problem-solution headline

  o Typically, start with a verb and BIG result from solution while evoking curiosity

- Explain big benefit subhead

  o Expand on your benefits; typically, use a series of additional benefits; tease to desire/solution

Section 2: Problem and Agitation

Focus on the problem your ideal customer is experiencing and amplify your understanding of it. Translation: Crank up the volume like pressing salt on a fresh wound.

Address possible objections head-on in this section using one or two bullets with the "if, then" approach.

Option One:

- If you want xyz so you will abc…

- If you want xyz so you will abc…

- If you want xyz so you will abc…

- Then efg is for you.

Or Option Two:

- If you want xyz so you can abc, then efg is for you.

- Here's why: (List at least three or four reasons; see list of whys to answer below.)

- As a xyz entrepreneur/coach/etc., I understand the need/drive to xyz, xyz, and xyz.

(Build on the drive/need to solve that problem.)

Section 3: Concise Story

Use a story to demonstrate the problem. Share the pivotal moment (a key lesson or discovery) which leads to solution.

Choose one type of story: creation, historical, parable, cautionary tale, etc.

- Start by framing the problem.

  o State the problem your solution solves.

○ Use a brief story that the reader will immediately connect to their goals.

- **Showcase the aha moment.**

  Show the epiphany and pivotal moment that drives to a key discovery.

- **Introduce the solution.**

  Highlight how the solution is useful, ultra-specific, and unique.

Section 4: Benefits

Most people buy when you answer WHY your solutions will:

- make and save money.
- avoid pain and gain comfort.
- improve health.
- help them feel loved or praised.
- save time and effort.

State what it is and what it does; answer WHY.

- How it works
- WHY it works
- What it includes

Section 5: Testimony

Hear what product users say.

- Include around THREE one- to two-sentence soundbites endorsing the transformation your solution created for them.

- Include a headshot of each person with first/last name and title or company.

Section 6: Pricing

- Set a price anchor: This typically costs xyz.
- Reveal the price.
- Cite your guarantee.
- Include bonuses (if you have them).
- Call to Action (Buy Button)

Section 7: Why Act Now

- Only use genuine scarcity; don't make up scarcity.
- Give reasons why they should take action.
- List the fork in the road:

  Option 1: Do nothing and continue xyz OR Option 2: Take action and experience this amazing transformation.

- Call to Action (Buy Button)

Section 8: Objections/FAQ

- Use this section to address objections in your customer's mind before they ask the question.
- List FAQs.
- Include call to action (buy button).

Sales Page (Example 1)

XYZ Virtual EVENT as a Sales Page

Overview:

The following example uses actual copy written for a client. I modified some of the words to make it "client-neutral" while still giving you an idea about how to write a sales page.

Please use this as a guide to develop your own sales page. This is shared as an example only. Like the uniqueness of zebra stripes, copywriting is unique to the writer and easy to spot when it has been copied. This example is NOT shared for you to copy and should NOT be considered a roadmap.

Summary:

The request was to write copy that sells the benefits of paying $XX to join a XYZ Virtual Event.

Every sales page I write uses frameworks to hone in on the problem, emphasize it, offer a solution, show results with testimonials, state the offer clearly, and ask people to take action.

Bolding on keywords and phrases throughout is intentional. Using colors, spacing, graphic icons, etc., will help break up the copy while drawing the eye.

The headlines and subheads are written with multiple purposes, including:

- Drawing in the reader because it speaks to them specifically
- Allowing the reader to scan and understand the call to action

This is written as one long-form sales page, and section breaks for design purposes only.

You could also include:

- FAQs, but you would need to discuss what questions you typically receive and the answers.

- A guarantee, but you need to discuss what to include for an event guarantee.

- Additional objections, but you would need to map out what objections you typically receive before addressing them in the copy.

HERO SECTION 1:

HEADER IMAGE: Logo top right overlay on a greyed-out image with the following text:

(example lead — eyebrow copy)

ATTENTION: If you're a XYZ-describe your audience, this special invitation is for you...

(example headline)

How to Move Your XYZ, and Make ABC While DEF

(subhead)

Join our next online XYZ-Event where faith, business, and XYZ business owners fit together.

(Add bold CTA button on the bottom of the image OR right below it.)

Sign Up for the Next XYZ-Event Today! <——CTA button copy

(Link the CTA button to jump to the place on the page where sign-up details or offers are listed)

SECTION 2:

(example paragraph copy)

If you're a **XYZ entrepreneur** looking for business buzz strategies...

If you're a **business owner** who longs to connect with like-minded women...

If you're a **sales professional** who wants to thrive in business while growing your faith...

Then the XYZ-Event will meet your needs while exceeding your expectations.

(subhead)

Do You Get Stretched Thin by Wearing Too Many Hats?

(example paragraph copy)

Like most XYZ descriptor of audience...

- Maybe you're so busy running your business and managing your family that it is hard to get it all done.

- Perhaps selling makes your palms sweat, so you avoid sales conversations whenever possible.

- Maybe you're flying by the seat of your pants without a strategic plan.

- Possibly you're struggling to generate new, money-making ideas and need a reliable, trustworthy sounding board.

- Even worse, you may constantly battle to live your faith while showing up in the marketplace.

SECTION 3:

(example subhead)

Experience Amazing Results OR Keep Things the Same: You Choose

(example paragraph copy)

Decisions are a part of life. No matter what you do—in life or business—you're always forced to decide between "thing" one and "thing" two.

Right now, you have a choice. Will you choose to:

- **Build confidence, learn, and grow** OR stay stagnant with a business-limiting mindset?

- **Put systems and processes in place** OR struggle juggling chaos without seeing results?

- **Let your supportive tribe lift you up** OR wallow in self-pity because your business is a one-XYZ shop?

- Find creative ways to overcome obstacles OR continue hitting roadblocks?

- **Take action to attend the next XYZ-Event** OR sleep on your decision, and wonder what you've missed?

As a female business owner, you know that getting things done is the only way to achieve success.

You have a choice to make: move forward or stay the same.

Choose to level up when you connect with this dynamic group of XYZ audience now.

Attend your first ABC-event, and let us show you how to reach your potential.

(Large, bold, CTA Button)

Yes! Book My XYZ-Event Now

(Link the CTA button to jump to the place on the page where sign-up details or offers are listed)

SECTION 4:

(example subhead)

Some Business Women Are Experiencing ABC, EFG, and XYZ. Are You?

(paragraph copy)

Let's face it; every day presents new challenges, from finding customers and dealing with the unknown to loneliness and self-doubt.

What if you could...

- Eliminate isolation with connections that help you achieve results in ALL aspects of your life and business?

- **Remove stressors** by learning how to **lean into God's Word** in all situations?

- Embrace your originality, so it fuels your business results and growth?

- Generate new ideas while sharpening your mindset and message?

- Expand your market while monetizing your creations and monitoring results?

SECTION 5:

(example subhead)

Give Us ##-Minutes & We'll XYZ Your Week

(example paragraph copy)

While every xyz-event is unique, our weekly meetings begin at exactly XX a.m. XYZ-Time Zone following this five-part outline:

Segment One: Get XYZ

You'll get inspired and go deeper as we open each XYZ-Event with ABC and dive into the EFG for practical application. The XYZ-specific activity will also help you focus on ABC, DEF, and XYZ.

Segment Two: Get XYZ

You'll **take your next steps with ABC** designed to help you **DEF**. During these ## minutes, you will **ABC, DEF,** and XYZ to gain clarity.

SECTION 6:

Consider breaking up background color by starting a new section to help text flow and draw the eye.

(example paragraph copy continued)

Segment Three: Get XYZ

You'll **network with other like-minded ABC** through structured XYZ connections. **Grow your connections** as each XYZ member shares introductions, ah-ha moments.

Segment Four: Get XYZ

You'll be ABC, DEF, HIJ, and KLM as we discuss how connecting in the XYZ helps you move forward to ABC. Experience how intertwined personal and professional lives will help you make an impact.

Segment Five: Get XYZ

You'll **learn key XYZ tips** when we unpack one of our XYZ-specific content.

Our interactive online XYZ-events are structured, so you will leave with XYZ-specific tools.

Click Here to Join Our Next XYZ-event<——Large, bold CTA

(Link the CTA button to jump to the place on the page where sign-up details or offers are listed)

SECTION 7:

(example subhead)

What Makes the XYZ-Event Different?

(testimonial copy with photos; instead of bullet points consider a creative way to layout the photos and quotes on the page)

- "one- to two-sentence testimony" ~insert name, photo
- "one- to two-sentence testimony" ~insert name, photo
- "one- to two-sentence testimony" ~insert name, photo
- "one- to two-sentence testimony" ~insert name, photo
- "one- to two-sentence testimony" ~insert name, photo
- "one- to two-sentence testimony" ~insert name, photo

SECTION 8:

(example subhead)

Are You Ready for A, B, and C That Will Lead to Your XYZ?

(example paragraph copy)

Get a glimpse into what you've been missing when attending **a XYZ-specific event.**

Invigorate your mindset when you join the next XYZ-event for just $XX. When you join us, you will:

- get ABC-specific want.
- get ABC-specific desire.
- get ABC-specific need.

- get ABC-specific opportunity.
- and so much more...

Sign Up Now. Register as our Guest for only $XX TODAY! (<——hyperlink to schedule section; CTA button)

SECTION 9:

Consider breaking up the background color by starting a new section to help text flow and draw the eye.

(example paragraph copy continued)

Each week we gather virtually to A, B, and C with other XYZ-specific audience.

Get your XYZ and ABC while you uncover XYZ and ABC.

If you want support and encouragement that lifts you higher, then the XYZ-event is for you.

Join a group where A, B, and C are XYZ!

SECTION 10:

Specific Result. Specific Result.

Specific CTA for the XYZ.

Come as you are from anywhere.

Join Our Next XYZ-Event for $XX!

($XX value)

Click the date that works best for you.

Register Now!

(Include CTA button options)

SECTION: 11

(example subhead)

First-Time XYZ-Event Attendees Frequently Ask…

Insert FAQs that answer specific questions and overcome objections people typically offer.

SECTION: 12

(example subhead)

Join Our Next XYZ-Event for $XX!

(That's a $XX value!)

Click the date that works best for you.

Register Now!

Insert specific date/time options

Sales Page Copy (Example 2)

Overview: The following example uses actual copy written for a client. I modified some of the words to make it "client-neutral" yet give you an idea about how to write a sales page. Please note that the (H1) indicates a html headline and (H2) indicates a html sub-headline.

Please use this as a guide to develop your own sales page. This is shared as an example only. It is NOT shared for you to copy and should NOT be considered a roadmap.

Name of Sales Page

Eyebrow (above opening headline, paragraph font)

Tired of chasing new XYZ solutions with LITTLE to NO success? Learn to ENHANCE what you're already doing for FREE. (details below)

Header section (Section 1):

Forget about XYZ and ABC (paragraph font)

XYZ Event Name (H1)

CTA Button: **Reserve Your Seat**

SECTION 2:

"I've tried all the latest tricks to make my XYZ and ABC grow, but trying to reach the right customers leaves me frustrated and anxious." *Sound familiar?*

Learn how successful ABC make DEF, save HIJ, and avoid extra KLM without chasing after the latest NOP, newest QRS, or shiny TUV.

SECTION 3:

Forget All the XYZ Hype (H2)

If your TIME is LIMITED and you're tired of ABC schemes.

If you're WEARY from constantly DEF what you do.

If someone else's HIJ methods are NOT working for you.

If you stay BUSY trying NEW strategies with LITTLE results.

If your KLM are growing, but your NOP aren't.

Then this **FREE XYZ** is for YOU!

Join us for **XYZ sessions** filled with ABC you will use on your XYZ immediately.

CTA Button: **Reserve Your Seat**

SECTION 4:

Are Things Going as You Planned? (H2)

As XYZ, we've all experienced moments in business where we think we're doing everything right, but something is off or keeps missing the mark.

Do you find yourself:

1. Studying what other ABC teach.
2. Buying the latest DEF.
3. Copying and revising HIJ others have written.
4. Implementing new KLM and NOP.
5. Searching for the QRS or TUV.
6. Building out WXY and ABC.
7. ABC and DEF LOTS of new GHI.
8. Creating JKL and MNO.
9. Posting PQR and offering a STREAM of STU.

But for whatever reason, **you just can't seem to ABC or get XYZ.** Everything you try seems to SUCK up a LOT of your time, and the desired **payoff for your efforts never appears.**

The dreams you envisioned have been replaced with ABC, DEF, and HIJ that you'll never grow your XYZ.

SECTION 5:

What If You Could Make a Few Tweaks and Experience Results? (H2)

Imagine what it would feel like to "figure it out" and **embrace that "aha moment" where you ABC confidently**, no matter what type of DEF or GHI you use.

Imagine how you'll start ABC because you've XYZ you were already doing.

Imagine using new ABC for ABC your XYZ, so you make any ABC as needed.

Imagine how you'll easily ABC that you need to make, so you're ABC.

Imagine confidently knowing what ABC will ABC and keep them ABC.

Imagine understanding what ABC looks like so well that you've stopped wasting time rethinking everything.

CTA Button: **Get Your XYZ.**

Reserve Your Seat Now.

SECTION 6:

Find the 'XYZ' of ABC (H2)

XYZ-Event attendees will hear best practices essential for any successful ABC.

Organized into **ABC sessions happening online weekly throughout ABC**, one of our experienced XYZ will offer you actionable steps and insights for:

- Addressing commonly overlooked ABC
- Writing the right ABC that XYZ
- Using ABC effectively in your XYZ
- Focusing on the ABC while avoiding XYZ
- Creating effective ABC
- Tips for ABC more and keeping your XYZ
- Insights for ABC
- Assessing what's ABC and what's not XYZ
- And so much more.

When you **register for** the low, low price of **FREE**, you'll get access to ALL ABC sessions (live and recorded), the workbook, giveaways, and so much more.

- **Ask questions** when you attend the online, LIVE sessions.

- **Review the Zoom recordings** online as much as you like.
- **Enhance your existing ABC** with easy-to-do exercises along the way.

CTA Button: **Reserve Your Seat**

SECTION 7 A AND B:

Join us for "XYZ-Event" and learn... (H2)

SESSION 1: Name, speaker, time Copy about the benefits of attending the session, share WIIFM (what's in it for me)	SESSION 2: Name, speaker, time Copy about the benefits of attending the session, share WIIFM (what's in it for me)
SESSION 3: Name, speaker, time Copy about the benefits of attending the session, share WIIFM (what's in it for me)	SESSION 4: Name, speaker, time Copy about the benefits of attending the session, share WIIFM (what's in it for me)

SECTION 8:

Your "XYZ" Speakers... (H2)

Headshot Speaker	Headshot Speaker	Headshot Speaker	Headshot Speaker
Speaker Name and Title	Speaker Name and Title	Speaker Name and Title	Speaker Name and Title
Company	Company	Company	Company

SECTION 9:

What Others Say… (H2)

"one- to two-sentence endorsement." ~name, company

"one- to two-sentence endorsement." ~name, company

"one- to two-sentence endorsement." ~name, company

SECTION 10:

Sign Up for XYZ-Event, 100% Risk-Free (H2)

Because we are confident these insights will help you enhance your XYZ, you can sign up for the entire ABC sessions for XZY.

The only thing you need to do is commit to improving **what you're already doing by** showing up, listening, and applying the lessons to your ABC.

Even if you can't make one of the sessions, you'll receive a link to the recordings that you may listen to at any time.

There's no hidden agenda or strings attached.

All you need to do is sign up, show up, and take action.

CTA Button: **Reserve Your Seat Now**

SECTION 11:

Couldn't You Just… (H2)

Turn objections into questions and then answer them. (Like a reverse FAQ.)

SECTION 12:

Why Not Level Up Your XYZ? (H2)

You're an XYZ with a ABC who needs to:

- Know how to XYZ and ABC

- Understand XYZ and ABC

- Learn how to XYZ and ABC

- Identify XYZ and ABC

Join us for "XYZ-EVENT."

With a XYZ, you have ABC.

CTA Button: **Reserve Your Seat Now**

What to Do After You Write

After you have written your copy, you want to apply and follow these steps.

- Run Your Copy Through Frameworks.

  - The Four U's
  - AIDA
  - Joyful Alignment Checklist
  - Ask for God's Help

- Follow These Tips.

  - Use Grammarly, not spellcheck.
  - Read your copy out loud (seriously).

    - This step will help you: find missing words, identify gaps, and see where clarity is missing.
    - Remember, computers can't find everything.

- Write with Active NOT Passive Voice.

- Write about THEM, Not You.

  - Write about your customer, their pain point, and how you solve it.

- Overcome Objections and Answer Why.

  - Make sure you've included these things in your writing.

- Use a Thesaurus.

  - Don't use the same words over and over again.

Isn't it exciting to know that you are a walking billboard for Christ? You can model Christlike characteristics to others in all you think, say, and do.

When you write marketing copy, use these tips to ensure your words sell, educate, and persuade joyfully without twisting reality.

Study and learn from others, but don't copy them. (Romans 12:2)

Elevate your God-given gifts. Show how you're unique. (Psalm 139:13–14)

Write clearly. Make what you are selling easy to understand. (Habakkuk 2:2)

- Use your audience's language.
- Overcome objections and answer why it will help them.
- Emphasize the benefits (not features) of what you offer.
- Show understanding using empathy and emotions.

Provoke emotions and motivate action without hype.

- **Reciprocity:** Give and get without hidden agendas, poor products, or strings attached. (Matthew 7:12)

- **Commitment:** Get customers to engage and agree with you about things that are true and right. (1 John 3:18)

- **Social Proof:** Make your proof points. You are God's social proof. (Matthew 5:16)

- **Authority:** Influence others without puffery or twisting the truth. Show your God-given abilities. (2 Corinthians 9:8) *Use active voice to show how your products "will" or "can" do something.*

Be Authentic. Don't manufacture desire for what you're selling.

Check what you write for alignment. Is what you've written joyful or hype-filled. If you find any hype, rewrite it to achieve alignment.

Joyful Copy Checklist

Joyful	Hype
Authentic, Pure	Dishonest, Embellished, Fake
Considerate, Gentle	Abrasive, Combative, Defiant
Genuine, Faithful	Hypocrisy, Insincere, Phony
Honest, Right	Corrupt, Fraudulent, Inaccurate
Honorable, Noble	Devious, Dishonest, Unethical
Integrity, Good	Deceitful, Manipulative, Trickery
Joy	Depressed, Negative
Kindness	Harsh, Hostile, Thoughtless
Love	Anger, Fear, Selfishness
Patient, Easy-Going	Cynical, Impatient, Vengeful
Peaceful	Anxious, Apathetic, Worrisome
Pleasant, Lovely	Agitated, Gloomy, Offensive
Praiseworthy, Admirable	Loathsome, Repulsive, Shameful
Self-Controlled	Impulsive, Manipulative, Hype

APPENDIX

A s a recap, let's revisit how to use this appendix as an ongoing resource. *The How-to Guide Power Tools* include my paraphrase of specific verses used in each chapter. While I wrote the paraphrases to emphasize what God placed on my heart, I strongly encourage you to read each verse in the actual Bible. I recommend that you read each verse in several translations to gain a deeper understanding of what they mean.

The translations I reference frequently include the New King James Version (NKJV), New International Version (NIV), and the Amplified Bible (AMP). On occasion, I'll also use The Message (MSG), the New Living Translation (NLT), and the Good News Translation (GNT). While everyone has reasons to favor one translation over another, I recommend you find what works best for you to understand what God is teaching through His Word (aka The Ultimate How-To Guide.)

The YouVersion Bible app, which is free, is accessible via the mobile app or your Internet browser at www.bible.com.

The Key Principles from each chapter are listed for quick and easy reference. I encourage you to read through them periodically to keep them top of mind.

The Joyful Copy Challenge: Ultimately, joyful copy is a reminder and challenge to partner with God before you write, throughout the writing process, and after you've written. The *Joyful Copy* Checklist is a visual reminder to filter everything you write, think, and say through Galatians 5:22–23 and Philippians 4:8. Whenever a phrase or thought is out of alignment, the goal is to revise it until it emulates Christian characteristics.

Have Questions? If you have questions about writing joyful copy, talk to God about it first. He may help you see what you need to change automatically. He may also point you to me. In that case, please email me at Joy@JoyCapps.com, and I'll get back to you as soon as possible.

Introduction: How-To Guide Power Tools

God's Word is our Ultimate How-To Guide. The Scriptures address many different situations in life and business. One of the best ways to get guidance and direction is by memorizing verses so that you can lean into them anytime. You'll find it easy to claim them over your life and business on demand when you have them memorized.

[PRO TIP] Write the verses on notecards and post-it notes. Carry them with you and put them in strategic places you frequent so you see them often.

God's plans for you are for your well-being and not adversity, so you have a future and hope. (~Jeremiah 29:11, Joy's Paraphrase)

You will find God when you seek Him consistently in all things, moment by moment, every day. (~Jeremiah 29:13, Joy's Paraphrase)

If you fill your life with a moment-by-moment partnership with God, His reality, initiatives, and provisions will meet your every need. Don't worry about missing out because God's got those who partner with Him. (~Matthew 6:33, Joy's Paraphrase)

Without a doubt, the One who created you to do good works will carry you through until the day the Lord returns. (~Philippians 1:6, Joy's Paraphrase)

Worrying and being anxious gets you nowhere fast. Praise God for what He's already done, then take all your concerns to the Lord in prayer. (~Philippians 4:6, Joy's Paraphrase)

Whatever you focus on will influence how you think, communicate, and act. (~Proverbs 23:7a, Joy's Paraphrase)

God gives those who follow Him power, love, and discernment—not fear. (~2 Timothy 1:7, Joy's Paraphrase)

Part I How-To Guide Power Tools: What Is Copy?

Add these additional verses to your arsenal and consider memorizing them.

[PRO TIP] Focus on one or two verses each week. Write them in your journal and ask God questions about each verse as you meditate on them. He wants to share with you, but He's waiting for you to spend time seeking, listening, and responding to Him.

God's Word was established before anything else and used as the foundation for everything He created. God's Word remains consistent and unchanging because it represents who He is. (~John 1:1, Joy's Paraphrase)

The Good News of salvation gives us God's power, authority, and the deep conviction of Holy Spirit. (~1 Thessalonians 1:5a, Joy's Paraphrase)

Find ways to encourage others to give and receive love and do Christ-like things. (~Hebrews 10:24, Joy's Paraphrase)

Smooth talkers intentionally twist words, manipulating naive people into actions and thoughts. Don't be deceived because those people are serving themselves, not God. (~Romans 16:18, Joy's Paraphrase)

Part I: Key Principles.

Copywriting uses words to connect any goods, services, or products with customers. Copywriting also educates and persuades.

Using words correctly will bring messages about anything to life—especially products and services that offer solutions to problems.

Knowing your audience well will help you use the right words to get prospects to take action.

The Bible is the Ultimate How-To Guide that teaches Christ-followers how to sell, persuade, and educate others.

Copywriting—when used correctly—pulls a common thread from beginning to end to encourage readers to take action.

Part II How-To Guide Power Tools: Defining *Joyful Copy*

Focus on these additional verses as you navigate your life and business.

[PRO TIP] Make the power of God's Word visible in your home and office. Select one or more Scriptures to focus on throughout each day and week. Consider writing it on a whiteboard or index card. Put it where you'll see it frequently. Practice saying it aloud.

Seek to emulate the fruits of the Spirit in every aspect of your life: love, joy, peace, patience, kindness, goodness, faithfulness, gentleness, and self-control. (~Galatians 5:22–23, Joy's Paraphrase)

Focus on things that are true, noble, right, pure, lovely, admirable and good, excellent, and praiseworthy. (~Philippians 4:8, Joy's Paraphrase)

Build your life and business on the firm foundation found only in Christ. If you build your world focused on any other thing, you'll experience temporary success that ends in failure. (~Matthew 7:24–27, Joy's Paraphrase)

We can love because He showed us love first. (~1 John 4:19, Joy's Paraphrase)

Love is patient, kind, and thoughtful. Love never shows envy or pride. It does not brag and is not arrogant. (~1 Corinthians 13:4, Joy's Paraphrase)

You'll experience joy when you give an appropriate answer at the right time. (Proverbs 15:23, Joy's Paraphrase)

Pain and sadness are only temporary because God's abiding joy will transform you after you've walked through sorrow. (Psalm 30:5, Joy's Paraphrase)

Seek God and learn to be like Him, and He'll take care of everything else. (~Matthew 6:33, Joy's Paraphrase)

Eliminate selfish ambition. Stop putting yourself first. Humble yourself and look for ways to help others. (~Philippians 2:3–4, Joy's Paraphrase)

Lift each other with encouraging, peaceful words. In turn, God's peace and love are with you. (~2 Corinthians 13:11, Joy's Paraphrase)

Turn everything over to God in prayer. When you do, His peace that is hard for most to understand will protect your heart and mind. (~Philippians 4:6–7, Joy's Paraphrase)

Don't grow tired of doing good because you'll produce results if you don't give up. (~Galatians 6:9, Joy's Paraphrase)

Take a stand for your faith in God in public. Don't hide it or try not to offend others by speaking the truth. (~1 Timothy 6:12, Joy's Paraphrase)

Don't share any corrupt or manipulative thoughts. Only share what will help, encourage, and benefit others. (~Ephesians 4:29, Joy's Paraphrase)

Do things that will promote spiritual well-being and bring blessing to other believers. (~Galatians 6:10, Joy's Paraphrase)

For the result of partnering with God generates goodness, righteousness, and truth. (~Ephesians 5:9, Joy's Paraphrase)

Jesus never moves or changes. He remains the same at any point in time—yesterday, today, and tomorrow. (~Hebrews 13:8, Joy's Paraphrase)

Gentle words melt anger while careless words stir the pot. (~Proverbs 15:1, Joy's Paraphrase)

Words of encouragement give life, but words that twist reality condemn and bring harm. (~Proverbs 15:4, Joy's Paraphrase)

Partner with God in everything you do (in life and business), and He will help you produce results you never imagined possible. (~Proverbs 16:3, Joy's Paraphrase)

Most of us plan what we're going to do, do it, and then ask God to bless it. But He's waiting for us to let go and partner with Him. (~Proverbs 16:9, Joy's Paraphrase)

During our time on earth, we are to stay focused on the faith, hope, and love God brings. But the greatest of those is love. (~1 Corinthians 13:13, Joy's Paraphrase)

Part II: Key Principles

Every aspect of a Christ-follower's life and business should strive to imitate godly characteristics found in God's Word, especially Galatians 5:22–23 and Philippians 4:8.

The deeper a tree's root structure goes, the more easily it will stand strong no matter what happens in the world around it. When a storm comes along, well-rooted trees with strong trunks remain intact through the ebb and flow of the elements around them.

Humans who focus on all the negative in the world tend to be insecure, anxiety-filled, walking train wrecks.

Christ-followers who are deeply rooted in God's Word, feed off the nutrients found in Scripture, and consistently seek a personal relationship with God are easy to spot. They usually have a spring in their step and an optimistic outlook on the world around them.

No matter who you are or what you do, your focus will influence how you think, communicate, and act.

God's Word (aka The Ultimate How-To Guide) recommends a laundry list of traits for God's children to think about, emulate, and share. Ideally, those same attributes will also show up in the words we write in our marketing and copywriting.

Many entrepreneurs leverage anxieties to get you to do whatever they want by weaving it into their marketing and copywriting.

Instead of pulling on the threads of fear, anger, shame, guilt, or selfishness—why not connect with customers by offering a choice between positive transformation and keeping the status quo.

As you write joyful copy for your business, you will want to pull on the thread of love and use fear only when it is authentic, genuine, and real.

Biblical joy is dependent on who Jesus is and not what is happening around us. Godly joy comes from Holy Spirit guiding us in all we think, say, and do each day.

If you want to stand out in today's noisy marketplace, the last thing you want to do is look like everyone else.

One of the easiest ways to get noticed is by focusing on others before yourself. Help others without expectations. Those who focus on their customers before themselves achieve results. Prospective clients seek out your business because of the transformation your solutions bring to whatever problem or pain they are experiencing.

When you write about your customers' problems and challenges that you know how to solve, point to the benefits they might be overlooking. Make sure every single stumbling block you point out shines the light on the beneficial blessings they will experience.

Choose to build a world filled with God's love, radiating peace and showcasing leadership. If you want to achieve long-lasting results in your business, you need to practice a balance between urgency and patience in every piece of marketing and copywriting. Writing about your business to connect with your audience requires patience and self-discipline.

Writing in alignment with the teachings of God's Word might require you to take an extra step or invest more time than you planned. But the payoff is worth it, especially when others realize you're shining God's light in today's dark world.

Problems arise when we use kindness to manipulate people into repaying "favors." Authentic kindness is filled with genuine truths. It isn't copied, false, or artificial. It isn't the type of kindness that someone made up just to get someone to do something. We need to strive to demonstrate kindness the way God did. In whatever copy you write and marketing you execute, display authentic kindness backed by ethical, non-manipulative behavior. Humans cannot display goodness the way God does without His help.

To display pure, godly goodness through our lives, businesses, marketing, words, actions, and deeds, we need to rely on Holy Spirit to guide and direct us. You might see goodness in our actions and words, but our hearts must be pure to demonstrate the goodness of Christ in our lives every day. To display God's pure goodness through what you write about your business, you have no choice but to invite Holy Spirit into what you're doing.

Write with sincerity and honesty. Let your integrity and God-like character shine through brightly.

Faithfulness is cultivated from the inside out. It is a daily discipline that shows up in our lives by being diligent over time. Faithful, Christ-following entrepreneurs will never seek to cut corners, cheat others, or act unjustly.

Gentleness is interwoven with all the other spiritual characteristics we are called to display in our lives.

Anyone can fake humility while arrogance and pride fill their heart. Genuine humility starts in the heart and generates gentleness that we display to others. No ego is involved. Gentle humility takes us off center stage and helps us influence others through the lens, strength, and power of Holy Spirit.

Our mission as Christ-followers, should we choose to accept it, is to start practicing self-control and let our "yes" mean yes and our "no" mean no. In our business, marketing, actions, words, and deeds, self-control should be more than a figure of speech. When we realize we have an option to turn control of things, people, situations, and actions over to God—and we let go and let God be in charge of every aspect of our world—that is when transformation happens.

- Apply liberal amounts of "holy duct tape."
- Don't dangle (self-serving) carrots in front of prospects.
- Focus on the value your solutions bring others.
- Stop creating false urgency with fictitious deadlines.

God calls you to infuse the words you write and the solutions you create as a Christ-follower with His faith, hope, and love. Your marketing copy should shine the light on all of the fruits of the Spirit and more, but especially love.

Part III How-To Guide Power Tools: Why Do You Need *Joyful Copy*?

Add these additional verses to your arsenal and consider memorizing.

[PRO TIP] As you study each of the verses, ask the Lord to point out an area you need to work on improving in your life and business. Once you have one or two areas, be intentional and focus on making the necessary changes.

Trust God with every aspect of your life, mind, and heart. Do not rely on your own insights. Recognize God moving in everything. When you do, He will show you what to do and where to go, and He will direct your steps. (~Proverbs 3:5–6, Joy's Paraphrase)

Seek godly wisdom by asking Him to fill and renew you with His wisdom and discernment. When you do, He will give you wisdom in abundance. (~James 1:5, Joy's Paraphrase)

Keep away from any evil. Even if there are subtle nuances and you think you can be strong, step away and don't allow any opportunity for it to impact your life, heart, or mind. (~1 Thessalonians 5:22, Joy's Paraphrase)

If you say yes, mean it. If you say no, stick with it. Don't waiver. (~Matthew 5:37a, Joy's Paraphrase)

Whatever you focus on and think about is what will come out in your words and actions. (~Proverbs 23:7a, Joy's Paraphrase)

Don't gossip or spread lies. (~Exodus 23:1a, Joy's Paraphrase)

God hates and will not tolerate proud looks, lying tongues, murdering others, wicked schemes, those who seek to do evil, consistently lie, even subtly, or a busybody who likes to stir the pot with friends, colleagues, and strangers. (~Proverbs 6:16–19, Joy's Paraphrase)

You will never see a lie come from the truth. (~1 John 2:21c, Joy's Paraphrase)

Never take advantage of others or do them wrong in any way. (~Leviticus 25:17, Joy's Paraphrase)

Gaining wealth created by lying won't last and leads to death. (~Proverbs 21:6, Joy's Paraphrase)

Be careful that the lies and deceitfulness of someone else do not mislead you. (~Matthew 24:2, Joy's Paraphrase)

Trust, once broken, is hard to regain. It is fragile like a spider's web and difficult to rebuild. (~Job 8:14a, Joy's Paraphrase)

Part III: Key Principles

Here are the critical principles addressed in each chapter found in Part III.

Key Principles: Chapter 14–16

If you lean into godly wisdom and discernment as you navigate life and business, you'll learn how to cut through the noise while holding your head high.

As everyone around you cranks up the volume with lies, deceit, and distorted truths, you must choose whether your marketing copy will align with the Bible or look like everyone else's.

Using psychology to create desire started shortly after God created man.

Whatever or whoever dominates your focus will control what you say and do.

Many use the psychology of words to creep into your head and take up residence without you even knowing it.

Negative and positive thoughts—whether real or not—cause people to act based on how those words made them feel.

Using emotions to create a false sense of desire or fake need for whatever you are selling is deceptive.

Key Principles: Chapter 17

Many marketers and entrepreneurs—even some who profess to be Christians—use emotions and principles of persuasion to sell you things you don't need.

If you're a Christ-following marketer or business owner, then you will strive to create genuine connections with your customer's EXISTING and REAL needs in mind.

Scarcity tactics are wrong or unethical when you use them to manipulate someone to take unnecessary action.

Reciprocity: The concept of "I'll scratch your back if you scratch mine" is okay if we use it with good intent and follow the Golden Rule. Problems arise when we use reciprocity to manipulate people into repaying "favors."

Commitment and Consistency: The concept of having skin in the game makes someone more invested. Problems arise when we use commitment and consistency to mislead intentionally.

Social Proof: Human psychology finds most people follow the actions of the masses. But using fake social proof to misrepresent or inflate reality is wrong.

Likeability: The more someone likes you and sees what they have in common with you, the easier it is for you to persuade them to do something. There's nothing wrong with stating your commonalities, as long as what you share is true.

Authority: Human nature typically respects perceived expertise, status, or power—whether it is real or not. If you're not an expert in something, don't use puffery or stretch the truth in an attempt to strengthen your position.

Scarcity: What is hard to come by or exclusive draws most everyone. Scarcity becomes twisted when FOMO or limited-time offers are not real. If you set a limit, threshold, or deadline—make sure it is authentic.

Key Principles: Chapter 18

Repetition = Truth

The more someone hears an idea, the easier it is to understand and accept it as truth. The Bible teaches us not to claim lies as truth or circulate false information.

Rhyme-as-a-Reason Effect

Some build trust by rhyming intentionally because most people are more likely to remember, repeat, and believe statements that end with similar sounds. Using the human psyche against other humans to per-suade and manipulate, while common, is not aligned with biblical prin-ciples.

Because

Giving people a reason for doing something typically results in their "compliance." The key is providing genuine reasons, not fabricated ones designed to serve your needs.

Headlines

Headlines are used in copy like a hook to draw in customers. Atten-tion-grabbing headlines are not wrong if they intrigue readers without misrepresenting the content behind the statement.

When someone manipulates a reader with twisted reality or hype that doesn't offer the promised value, it can and will negatively impact a brand, business, or individual.

Part IV How-To Guide Power Tools: *Joyful Copy* Is Not a Blueprint

Add these additional verses to your arsenal and consider memorizing.

[PRO TIP] Consider reading through each verse at least three times. As you say it, reflect on how you can live out what each passage says. Ask God to point out how He would have you live out the Scripture in your business.

Stop copying others to gain success or fit in. Instead, let God trans-form who you are and how you show up in the world. When you strive to partner with Him, He will show you what He wants you to do, far better than you could ever imagine. (~Romans 12:12, Joy's Paraphrase)

Use whatever gifts you have received to serve others. (~1 Peter 4:10, Joy's Paraphrase)

Just as you can identify a tree by its fruit, you can identify people by their actions. (~Matthew 7:20, Joy's Paraphrase)

This entire passage in Ephesians is good for meditation, but these few points jump out to me as part of the Ultimate How-To Guide God calls us to follow. (~Ephesians 5:1–10, Joy's Paraphrase)

- Imitate God in everything you do. (*Not some things, but all things.*)
- Obscene stories, foolish talk, and coarse jokes are not for you.
- Greedy people worship the things of this world.
- Don't be fooled by those who rationalize their sins.
- Living in the light of God will produce what is good, right, and true.
- Determine what pleases God and do that.

Those who partner with God in all they do will strive to emulate, with the help of Holy Spirit, the biblical characteristics of love, joy, peace, patience, kindness, goodness, faithfulness, gentleness, and self-control. (~Galatians 5:22–23, Joy's Paraphrase)

Fill your minds with those things that are good and that deserve praise: things that are true, noble, right, pure, lovely, and honorable. Focus on good, truthful, dignified, right, pure, lovely, and honorable things. (~Philippians 4:8, Joy's Paraphrase)

God will bless those who hear His Word and strive to obey it in all aspects of their life and business. (~Luke 11:28, Joy's Paraphrase)

Part IV: Key Principles

This section addresses the key principles found in Part IV.

God's Word is clear that we are not to copy others.

Copying someone else jumps right over and ignores Abba Father's specific plans for your life. Why shortchange yourself of the blessings

God has planned for you simply because you pursued "a shortcut" by copying someone else's blueprint?

Ethical copy, aka joyful copy, follows the guiding principles found in God's Word about how we should think, speak, and act.

God's principles are not ala carte options.

If you align your business with the teachings of the Bible, then your words will convey truthfulness and hope without stretching or twisting reality. Your business will use joyful copy.

If you want your copy to be ethical and joyful, filter what you've written through Scripture.

Take the time to review what you've created and written. Check to see if your copy, content, courses, books, products, and services are joyful. If you find any form of hype, take the necessary steps to make it right.

Anyone who claims to be a Christ-follower and lives by the teachings of the Bible should never use an ounce of hype or manipulation in their words, deeds, or actions.

Trust is so important in life and business that you need to make sure you deliver what you say you're going to give someone. And make sure you buy products, services, and solutions from people who will keep their word, too.

Be careful not to follow the breadcrumb trail someone leaves you because you think it will make you wealthy.

Do not copy someone else's roadmap because they promise it will increase your email list or finances.

If you feel the need to follow a roadmap, turn to the God-inspired roadmap (aka the Bible and Ultimate How-To Guide) and ask Holy

Spirit to guide you. While you're at it, ask Him to give you strategies and frameworks that will help you get where He wants you to go.

Part V How-To Guide Power Tools: How to Determine Copy that Connects

God filled the Bible with verses you and I can rely on as our power tools and how-to guide. Here are more Scriptures that will help you in your journey.

[PRO TIP] Some verses will speak to you louder than others. Partner with Holy Spirit to help you select which of the following verses to memorize.

If you put all your focus, trust, and hope in God, you replenish your strength and power. (~Isaiah 40:31, Joy's Paraphrase)

Be alert and aware because the evil one is sneaky and continually looking for ways to trip you up and suck you into his twisted world of lies. Don't give the devil a foothold because he will eat you up without you realizing what he's doing. (~1 Peter 5:8, Joy's Paraphrase)

Every single activity in life has a season and time to happen. (~Ecclesiastes 3:1, Joy's Paraphrase)

Planning is good, but realize God will have the last word. (~Proverbs 16:1, Joy's Paraphrase)

God created you to do good works. He planned out what He wanted you to do before He created you in your mother's womb. (~Ephesians 2:10, Joy's Paraphrase)

We are all to use our skills and talents to create what God needs and has asked us to do. Be obedient. (~Exodus 35:10, Joy's Paraphrase)

God is responsible for sending every good gift your way. He is the Creator of all things who remains constant and never varies. (~James 1:17, Joy's Paraphrase)

Asking God for something with the wrong motives will not produce results. (~James 4:3, Joy's Paraphrase)

Praise God joyfully in your heart, thoughts, and actions in all things. (~1 Peter 1:8c, Joy's Paraphrase)

Part V: Key Principles

With so many frameworks and how-to content included in Part V, I felt led to keep the key principles recap light by pulling out just a few points.

The best way to start anything is by posturing and partnering with God, then following His lead to design what you'll create.

Before you work on any project:

- Talk to God about it.

- Ask Him to fill and renew you with His Holy Spirit, help you hear His voice in ALL you think, say, and do, and help you take action on it.

- Be intentional to do what Holy Spirit impresses on you to do.

Reflect and pray about each step you take as you work through writing joyful copy.

Use heavenly wisdom and discernment as your filter and guide when you navigate through life, work on your business, and strive to write joyful copy.

Use the knowledge you uncover to position your business strongly and strategically. Ask Holy Spirit to help you use this information to see things you haven't recognized in the past.

Ask Holy Spirit to help you see which items you should elevate and focus on. Also, ask Him to point out topics you should avoid. Invite the Lord into what you're doing, and listen.

Your answer to potential objections will always align with the teachings of the Bible. You will never answer with subtle hype or promises you never plan to fulfill.

The more knowledge you uncover about potential objections, the better prepared you'll be to address the concerns BEFORE customers mention them.

If you align your marketing copywriting with the teachings of the Bible, God will use your words to penetrate hearts and minds. I firmly believe He will also bring your copy to mind and help people think of you when the time is right for them.

Make sure what you're planning to say fits into God's design for your business and what you share is in complete alignment with the teachings of the Bible without twisting reality to get people to act.

Since God IS the Creator who made you, He will give you better insights about what unique things you should elevate through your business than any human.

Part VI How-To Guide Power Tools: Distill *Joyful Copy*: Connecting with Your Customers

By now, you understand how powerful God's Word is in all aspects of your life and business. Here are some more How-to Guide Power Tools (aka Scripture verses) to add to your ammunition box.

Don't do anything out of selfish motives, gains, or vanity. Instead, be humble and put others' interests above your own. (~Philippians 2:3–4, Joy's Paraphrase)

In everything you do, give your best effort for the Lord. Remember to work for God's glory, not the success or glory of others. (~Colossians 3:23, Joy's Paraphrase)

Ask for God's will, and He will give it to you. Seek God's direction, blessings, and provision, and you'll find He opens the right doors and opportunities for you. (~Luke 11:9, Joy's Paraphrase)

If you know what is right to do but aren't obedient, you're sinning against God. (~James 4:17, Joy's Paraphrase)

Get your mind, heart, and soul ready for action by being sober in spirit, using self-discipline, and leaning into God's strength. Stay focused on God, so you'll know when Jesus arrives. (~1 Peter 1:13, Joy's Paraphrase)

Be doers of the word, and not hearers only, deceiving yourselves. Do what God's Word says. If you don't take action on what God's Word says, you're misleading yourself. (~James 1:22, Joy's Paraphrase)

If you seek out God in all you think, say, and do, He will come closer to you. (~James 4:8, Joy's Paraphrase)

Seek to emulate the fruits of the Spirit in every aspect of your life: love, joy, peace, patience, kindness, goodness, faithfulness, gentleness, and self-control. (~Galatians 5:22–23, Joy's Paraphrase)

Focus on things that are true, noble, right, pure, lovely, admirable and good, excellent, and praiseworthy. (~Philippians 4:8, Joy's Paraphrase)

Stop being focused on yourself. Focus on the interests of others instead. (~ 1 Corinthians 10:24, Joy's Paraphrase)

Part VI: Key Principles

Here is a quick reference to the key principles mentioned in Part VI.

Whatever you write, focus on THEM, not YOU.

Helping others will drive your success. The key is to do for others without expecting anything in return.

When you put yourself last, you WILL stand out because everyone else is me-centric and copying what they see others do.

Living life according to the teachings of the Bible AND good copywriting uses JOY: JOY = Jesus First, Others Second, Yourself Last.

You are guaranteed to get someone's attention when you start talking about their problems, wants, desires, or needs.

Active voice will also make your tone more conversational, which is another key to writing engaging copy that connects with your audience.

When it comes to shining God's light in the world, you need to take action. Likewise, follow what the Ultimate How-To Guide models by writing copy using active voice.

You'll achieve success when you figure out where you're going and how to get there before you embark on your journey.

Before you write any words to build awareness or promote your solutions, you need to start with the end in mind.

You'll experience greater success when you invite Holy Spirit into the process at the very beginning.

ABOUT THE AUTHOR

With a heart to serve others, Joy helps entrepreneurs, business owners, and small-to-medium-sized businesses from a variety of industries use ethical marketing, joyful copy, and values-based business coaching to connect with their customers. Over the past 20+ years, Joy has provided marketing, public relations, and copywriting services to an array of clients who include well-known brands you've heard of and little-known brands you may never encounter.

As a creative problem-solver and Kingdom Driven Entrepreneur Certified Service Provider, Joy offers Done-WITH-You and Done-FOR-You services to help entrepreneurs—like you—show up in today's marketplace authentically without twisting reality. Joy also offers Joyful Copy 1-on-1, group coaching, and courses, and she speaks to groups regularly about ethical copywriting. Reach out to Joy at Joy@JoyCapps.com and visit her website at www.joycapps.com.

Joy balances everything by weightlifting, kayaking, and scuba diving with her husband, Robert. She also spends a lot of time receiving love and entertainment from their two fur-sons, Paisley and Finley (aka Cavalier King Charles Spaniels). As a family, they recently relocated from Charleston, South Carolina to Land O Lakes, Florida to live near Joy's mother.

www.ingramcontent.com/pod-product-compliance
Lightning Source LLC
Chambersburg PA
CBHW071138130626
46553CB00004B/1420